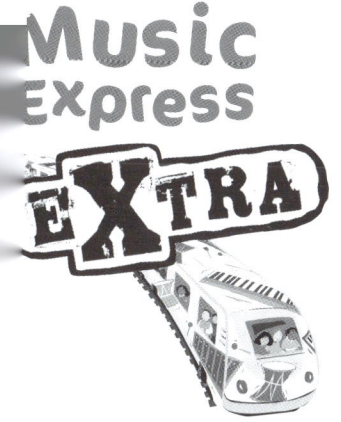

Developing music skills

Musical confidence for beginners –
activities for teaching general musicianship

Stephen Chadwick and Maureen Hanke

Illustrated by
Alison Dexter

A&C Black • London

Introduction

Music Express EXTRA: Developing Music Skills is an inspiring, imaginative and comprehensive music resource for generalist and specialist teachers, instrumental teachers and children. It is designed to teach the essential musical skills of beat, rhythm and pitch to all children, and is particularly helpful to those at the pre-instrumental stage of learning.

The resource will help form a perfect curriculum of general musicianship activities for the classroom and is particularly appropriate for children gaining access to instrumental tuition in whole class situations.

Each activity is self contained and all begin with listening. The activities can and should be re-visited regularly because these essential musical skills need repeated practice. They are also able to support other musical skills:

• Listening • Aural memory • Structure • Expression • Notation • Singing • Performing

HOW THE PACK IS ORGANISED AND WHAT YOU NEED

Book

The book is in two parts. The first, *Skill builders*, concentrates on experiencing, practising and internalising beat, rhythm and pitch. The second part, *Celebrate!*, focuses on performance and provides opportunities to apply the skills learnt in the first part of the book in a slightly broader and more challenging context.

▶ The **Play** sign in the *Skill builder* instructions indicates that the corresponding track for the activity needs to be played.

⬜ The **Stop play** sign in the *Skill builder* instructions indicates that some work needs to be done without the corresponding track.

CD/CD-ROMs

The two CD/CD-ROMs are both enhanced CDs. Use them in a conventional CD player in order to play the audio tracks. Use them on a computer/whiteboard set up in order to show the children the whiteboard displays or to make printouts. The whiteboard displays contain embedded audio – click the CD icon on the display page in order to hear the relevant track. (The embedded audio files will run on most versions of Acrobat Reader but the sound quality will depend on your computer sound system; it may be preferable or necessary to use the conventional audio tracks provided.)

CD/CD-ROM 1

• CD audio tracks for *Skill builders* (track list inside back cover)

• Whiteboard colour displays for *Celebrate!* with optional embedded MP3 audio.

• Printouts – the whiteboard displays may be printed out and photocopied as an alternative to using a whiteboard and for children to work with independently.

CD/CD-ROM 2

• CD audio tracks for *Celebrate* (track list inside back cover)

• Whiteboard colour displays for *Skill builders* with optional embedded MP3 audio.

• Printouts – the whiteboard displays may be printed out and photocopied as an alternative to using a whiteboard and for children to work with independently.

Additionally you will need a range of common classroom percussion instruments for the *Celebrate* section, eg xylophones, claves, wood block, tambourine.

Skill builders

There are 36 activities in this section. Use each of them as many times as you like, giving the children plenty of opportunities to repeat each of the three levels of difficulty for each activity. Gradually move on to the next activity: each is progressively harder than the one before, or teaches a different aspect of musical confidence.

The activities focus on listening, copying and movement. Further reinforcement is then provided through various types of graphic notation which progress to traditional staff notation. (The use of traditional staff notation is left to the teacher's discretion – the pack provides opportunities for using it, and introduces basic metres, rhythms and pitch notations progressively, but it does not set out to provide a comprehensive course in staff notation.)

BEAT The general aims of this section are to develop skill and confidence in:

- internalising the beat;
- keeping a steady beat;
- performing with accuracy on given beats;
- performing tasks of ever-increasing complexity and demand while keeping in time.

RHYTHM The general aims of this section are to develop skill and confidence in:

- responding to rhythm;
- developing rhythmic memory;
- performing rhythms with accuracy against a beat;
- understanding musical elements and notation;
- performing tasks of ever-increasing complexity and demand while keeping in time.

PITCH The general aims of this section are to develop skill and confidence in:

- responding to pitch;
- developing pitch memory;
- performing pitch with accuracy against another part;
- understanding musical elements and notation;
- performing tasks of ever-increasing complexity and demand.

Celebrate!

The seven performance pieces are progressively more demanding but all have very accessible starting points. Use them as many times as you like, giving the children plenty of opportunities to build familiarity with each piece and work towards a real celebration of musical skills and confidence.

THE PERFORMANCES

In each celebration, children learn a song or a piece of music through focussing on its beat, its rhythm patterns and its melodies and harmonies. When these aspects of the piece have been learnt and the children are completely familiar with them, they perform the piece, following the suggestions given or by creating their own performance plan.

Through this experience, children learn to listen carefully and with attention to detail, identifying and recalling musical patterns from memory, particularly developing their 'thinking voice'. They learn about playing together, blending instrumental sounds and to sing songs of increasing complexity in rounds and by adding a second vocal part. They are able to start simple improvisations, experimenting with melody and rhythm. They learn about the structure of a piece and have the opportunity to engage with simple music notation presented in appropriate and helpful, bite-sized chunks.

Contents

BEAT SKILL BUILDERS

1 Twos and fours   8
Contemporary grooves: marking beats 2 and 4 in 4-beat time.

2 Ping pong   9
Indian fusion: responding on the beat to randomly placed, aural cues.

3 Beat it   10
African and Latin: keeping the beat against a variety of straight and syncopated grooves.

4 Conducting   11
Classical fusion: conducting two beats to the bar; responding to dynamics.

5 Country chicken   12
USA Country: keeping time in 3-beat and 4-beat time.

6 Andean bird   13
Andean folk style: following changes in speed.

7 Beat box beats   14
Contemporary grooves: performing a steady beat in different subdivisions of 4-beat time; introducing basic notation.

8 Beat patterns   15
Electronic grooves: keeping the beat against syncopation and marking time when the beat is silent.

9 Cyborg chase   16
Contemporary grooves: performing several beat speeds together.

10 Rap split   17
Rap: performing on random beats; following a two-part and four-part score.

11 Time change   18
Electronic grooves: keeping time in 3-, 4- and 5-beat time.

12 Flamenco fever   19
Spanish fusion: performing and layering patterns made by leaving some beats silent; performing at a fast pace.

Teaching tips

You can approach these skill building activities in a number of different ways to ensure steady, secure development.

• Preparation time is designed to be brief, but it will be helpful to listen to the skill track before reading through the activity. This will familiarise you with the sounds and enable you to absorb the written instructions readily before presenting the activity to your pupils.

• Some teachers may like to lead from the whiteboard displays, using the book for extra support, others may like to work from the book, using the displays for occasional reference when notation is involved.

• In general, work through the beat, rhythm and pitch activities at the same time, eg you might focus on a level from Beat 1, Rhythm 1 and Pitch 1 over a three week period.

• Beat 1 develops the skills which provide a platform for Rhythm 1 and in turn Pitch 1.

• Each skill section has its own inbuilt progression, eg in performance complexity or musical understanding.

• Practising 5-10 minutes every other day is better than one half hour per week.

• Experienced children will be able to work through level 1-3 of one skill activity before moving on to the next. Less experienced children (and teachers) may simply complete level 1 of all the activities, then come back to revise and if appropriate move on to levels 2 and 3.

RHYTHM SKILL BUILDERS

1 Pop of the peeps   20
Contemporary grooves: imitating simple crotchet/quaver rhythms; reading from simple dot notation.

2 Taj Mahal Dancing   21
Indian fusion: imitating simple crotchet/quaver rhythms linked to word rhythms.

3 Slide it   22
African and Latin: imitating crotchet/minim rhythms; relating rhythm to beat.

4 Have a rest   23
Classical fusion: performing a simple crotchet/quaver rhythm; measuring and conducting rest bars.

5 Twang and crow   24
USA Country: imitating rhythms within 3-beat and 4-beat time; counting out rhythms while clapping.

6 Andean bird dance   25
Andean folk style: longer rhythmic phrases including crotchet rests performed with changes in tempo; performing ostinatos.

7 Beat box rhythms   26
Contemporary grooves: performing more complex rhythms using minims, crotchets, quavers and semi-quavers; relating these to beat; performing several rhythms together.

8 Syncopate it   27
Electronic grooves: performing off-beat and on the beat crotchet/quaver rhythms in sequence and combination.

9 Cyborg attack   28
Contemporary grooves: more syncopation; combining beat with rhythm in several parts.

10 Word walk   29
Rap: performing more complex sequences of rhythms related to words; performing two parts together.

11 Three four five   30
Electronic grooves: imitating rhythms within 3-, 4- and 5 beat time signatures; dotted crotchet and relationship to beat.

12 Castanet cuisine   31
Spanish fusion: imitating complex rhythms linked to word rhythms; working out rhythmic notation using crotchet, quaver, dotted quaver and semi-quavers.

Contents (continued)

PITCH SKILL BUILDERS

1 Line by line 32
Contemporary grooves: recognising basic pitch direction and relationship of up, down, high and low.

2 Ping pong pitch 33
Indian fusion: recognising and imitating simple pitch patterns.

3 Smooth it 34
African and Latin: recognising and imitating simple pitch patterns.

4 Pom pom pom 35
Classical fusion: reading and performing a sequence of simple pitch patterns.

5 Chicken pets 36
USA Country: recognising and imitating more complex pitch patterns; introducing the 5-line stave and letter names; basic part singing.

6 Andean bird song 37
Andean folk style: analysing pitch shapes within an extended phrase; basic part singing.

7 Beat box toonz 38
Contemporary grooves: recognising and performing short phrases; singing in four parts.

8 Martians 39
Electronic grooves: recognising and imitating more complex pitch patterns; listening for aural cues; part singing within a syncopated texture.

9 Cyborg hide and seek 40
Contemporary grooves: recognising and performing sequential pitch shapes; understanding that these can be moved higher or lower and still have the same shape; part singing.

10 Hill walk 41
Rap: following pitch movement over an extended phrase; singing in two parts.

11 Chemistry 42
Electronic grooves: recognising and imitating more complex pitch patterns in 3-, 4- and 5-beat time.

12 Food fiesta 43
Spanish fusion: identifying and performing longer pitch patterns; recognising a sequence of notated phrases.

CELEBRATE!

Number song
44

A playful brain teaser with numbered pitches. Sing it as written, jumble the numbers, perform it as a round.

Hi lo chicka lo
46

A clever clapping game to test co-ordination, co-operation and aural skills. Combine it with a *Country chicken* walk for a final performance.

Bodywork
48

Rhythms, beats, and body percussion – celebrate memory, co-ordination, and teamwork in an exciting percussion-only performance piece.

Hey, Mr Miller
50

A song which celebrates the excitement of playing instruments in big band, swing style.

Yonder come day
52

A three-part, uplifting fusion of song, chant and body percussion.

Saint train swing sing
54

A coming together of four great spirituals in a brilliant show-piece performance.

Ayalevi
56

A lively, welcoming, greeting song from Ghana, which combines movement, dance, percussion and joyful call and response singing.

Staff notation of melody lines   58
Acknowledgements   64
CD track list (see inside back cover)

Teaching tips

Approach these performance activities in whole or part, revisiting them as often as you like and with increasing confidence.

• It will be helpful to listen to the Celebrate! tracks before reading through the activity instructions. This will familiarise you with the sounds and enable you to absorb the written instructions readily before presenting the activity to your pupils.

• Some teachers may like to lead from the whiteboard displays, using the book for extra support, others may like to work from the book, using the displays for occasional reference when notation is involved.

• All the performances build on skills learnt in the beat, rhythm and pitch sections – a reference to each is located on the relevant page. These are for guidance only and are not unbreakable rules of progression.

• The performance section has its own inbuilt progression, but again this is not a hard and fast order which has to be followed.

• Practising 5-10 minutes every other day is better than one half hour per week.

• Experienced children will be able to work through the beat, rhythm and pitch activities and achieve an accomplished performance in a few sessions. Less experienced children (and teachers) may happily complete one part of each piece, eg the beat activity, then come back to revise and if appropriate move on to the rhythm and pitch activities.

Beat skill builder I ~ Twos and fours

Listen to Twos and fours

What you will need

1))) WB1-4

Level 1
WB1-2

▶ After the count in (12341234), all count the beat out loud throughout. Tap two fingers in the palm of the hand. Emphasise beats 2 and 4: 1**2**3**4** (WB1).

▶ Continue to count 1**2**3**4**, but clap on beats 2 and 4 (WB2).

I	2	3	4
	👏		👏

▶ Continue to clap beats 2 and 4, but internalise the count – count silently.

Level 2
WB3

▶ After the count in, clap on 2 and 4 as above. After four bars of clapping (1 **2** 3 **4** x 4), change to a different action on beats 2 and 4 for four bars. Clap again then change again:

1**2**3**4** x 4	1**2**3**4** x 4	1**2**3**4** x 4	1**2**3**4** x 4	1**2**3**4** x 4	1**2**3**4** x 4	1**2**3**4** x 4	1**2**3**4** x 4	1**2**3**4** x 4

Level 3
WB4

▶ Alternate these two movement sequences throughout:

1st sequence x 2:

I	2	3	4	I	2	3	4

2nd sequence x 2:

I	2	3	4	I	2	3	4

▶ For a real challenge, perform both sets of movements at the same time.

Teaching tips

Level 1: if the children find clapping on 2 and 4 difficult, let them make a silent gesture on the 1st and 3rd beats to help mark the time (eg pat the 'air' with hands wide apart between claps.)

Level 2: the change in action coincides with the change in drum pattern. The children will soon be able to feel when the change comes as they become familiar with the music.

The sequence of actions are suggestions only. You or a volunteer might lead any 4-bar sequence you like, or let everyone decide for themselves an action to alternate with clapping.

Level 3: each movement should be deliberate and quick, but not rushed.

Extension: try this game. Choose a volunteer to make a different sound or gesture on the 2nd beat of each bar (for example, clap hands, point to left, hold hand up, say 'beep'). The class copy the sound or gesture on the 4th beat.

The whiteboard displays for this and subsequent pages provide optional graphic support.

Beat skill builder 2 ~ Ping pong

2))) WB5-6

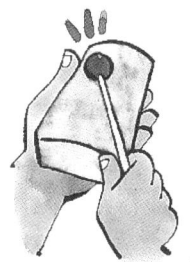

Listen to Ping pong

Questions you might ask

- What does the count in tell us about the music? (There are 4 beats to the bar.)
- What do you hear before the count in? (A finger cymbal then a wood block.)
- Do you hear them again anywhere? (Yes. They are heard throughout the music; first the finger cymbal sound is played a number of times, then the wood block sound plays a number of times and so on.)
- What else can you hear in the music? (Drums all through; each time you hear the finger cymbal or wood block sound there is a clap on the following beat.)

Level 1
WB5

▶ After the count in (12341234), all count the beat out loud throughout, gently tapping two fingers in the palm of the hand to feel the beat of the music.

Level 2
WB5

▶ Count silently but mark the beat by slightly nodding the head on each beat.

▶ When this is secure, everyone claps once on the beat after each finger cymbal or wood block sound.

Level 3
WB6

☐ Study the Indian dance positions below (WB6). Practise moving quickly from one position to another, holding each position like a statue.

▶ On the beat after each finger cymbal or wood block sound, change to another statue position.

Teaching tips

Level 2: to be ready to clap, the children should hold their palms lightly together so they can respond quickly.

If the children have a tendency to rush in with the clap, repeat level 1.

Extension game: divide the class into three groups.
Group 1 – clap as usual on the beat after the finger cymbal or wood block sound;
Group 2 – pat knees one beat after group 1;
Group 3 – stamp foot one beat after group 2.

Beat skill builder 3 ~ Beat it

Listen to Beat it

What you will need

3))) WB 7-10

Questions you might ask

- How many beats are there to the bar? (4.)

- What kind of music does it remind you of? (African; Latin American; a mixture of music from different places.)

- Quietly count the beat throughout as you listen carefully. What can you hear happening? (The music keeps changing; there are lots of different grooves; the groove lasts for four bars; there are ten grooves; the grooves get more and more off-beat and it gets harder to count the beat.)

Level 1   WB7-8

▶ After the count in (12341234), all quietly count the beat and gently tap it on palms (WB7).

▶ When secure, perform this sequence of actions to the beat, keeping each action going till the groove changes (WB8):

| Groove 1 | Groove 2 | Groove 3 | Groove 4 | Groove 5 |

| Groove 6 | Groove 7 | Groove 8 | Groove 9 | Groove 10 |

Level 2   WB9

▶ After the count in, say **Yeah** on every first beat. When the groove changes, the word changes:

Yeah	Me	You	What	No
Groove 1	Groove 2	Groove 3	Groove 4	Groove 5

Hey	Really	Bad	Say	Wow
Groove 6	Groove 7	Groove 8	Groove 9	Groove 10

Teaching tips
The piece is a collection and fusion of contemporary African and Latin American grooves. There are ten grooves.
Level 2: each word should be said quickly in the space of the first beat.

Level 3   WB10

▶ Perform the sequence of actions from Level 1 and call the words from Level 2 at the same time.

Beat skill builder 4 ~ Conducting

What you will need
4))) WB11-12

Listen to Conducting

Questions you might ask

- How many beats are there to the bar? (2.)

- Do you recognise any of the music? (The piece uses fragments of Beethoven's *5th Symphony*.)

- After the count in, another voice counts the beat. What happens to the counting? (It stops about half way through.)

- In some places there is complete silence; does the beat stop? (No, when the music comes back in it's still in time; you can carry on counting 1 2 through the silent bits; the beat can't be heard but it's still there keeping time.)

Level 1   WB11

▶ After the count in (1212), all quietly count the beat and gently tap it on palms. Even when the counting stops, keep counting and tapping the beat.

Level 2   WB12

▢ Demonstrate these conducting movements: move arm down for beat 1 and up for beat 2 (see *Teaching tips*).

▶ Give the class a little time to practise their conducting without the track. Next, play the track. The class conduct throughout after the count in.

Level 3

▶ In *Conducting* the music is made up of several contrasting sections in which the volume (dynamics) change. Listen together, noticing the dynamics:

Section	dynamics	counting
Introduction	Loud sustained notes	✔
A	Quiet tune building to climax	✔
B	Quiet tune building to climax	✔
C	Loud sustained notes	✔
A	Quiet tune building to climax	✘
B	Quiet tune building to climax	✘
C	Loud sustained notes	✘
Coda	Quiet tune suddenly ending loudly	✘

▶ Ask the children to make smaller conducting movements when the music is played quietly and larger ones when the music is loud. When the music becomes gradually louder, the class should make their arm movements gradually larger.

Teaching tips

Level 1: when counting the beat quietly, the children must keep the beat steady (particularly during periods where the music consists of long sustained notes).

Level 2: when conducting two beats to the bar, the end of the downward arm movement coincides with beat 1; the top of the upward arm movement coincides with beat 2:

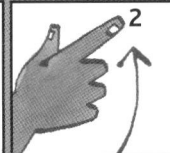

Encourage the children to count silently instead of out loud while conducting. Again, they must keep the beat steady even when the music is silent, so they do not go 'out of time'.

Level 3: the children will tend to conduct faster when the music gets louder and vice versa – remind them to keep the beat steady.

Beat skill builder 5 ~ Country chicken

Listen to Country chicken

What you will need

5))) WB13-15

Questions you might ask

- The music alternates between two contrasting sections. What do you notice about the difference between them? (One section features a banjo and has 3 beats to the bar; the other features harmonica and has 4 beats to the bar.)
- Is the tempo (speed) of the beat slow or fast? (It is quite slow.)

Level 1   WB13

▶ After the count-in (123123), all gently tap the beat on palms, noticing where the sections change, but continuing to tap.

Level 2   WB14

▶ Now count the beat as well as tapping it. In the 3-beat section, count 123 and emphasise the first beat by counting and tapping slightly louder:

1	2	3	x 8

In the 4-beat section, count 1234, again emphasising the first beat:

1	2	3	4	x 4

This all repeats, then the banjo section is played once more to end.

Level 3   WB15

▶ Perform these movements to the beat:

Chicken wing – in the 3-beat section the children pat their knees then squeeze their elbows in and out like a chicken flapping its wings.

x 8

Chicken strut – in the 4-beat section the children walk on the spot like a chicken and cluck on the first beat:

x 4

Teaching tips

Levels 2 and 3: the children may find the transition from section to section difficult at first and lose count of how many repetitions they have done. However, the more they listen to the music, the more naturally they will be able to 'feel' the structure and length of each section.

Beat skill builder 6 ~ Andean bird

What you will need

6))) WB16-18

Listen to Andean bird

Questions you might ask

- How many beats are there to the bar? (3.)

- There are four sections; each is introduced by a count in and gong. What do you notice about the sections? (In each section the tempo is different; section 1 is slow, section 2 speeds up, section 3 is fast and section 4 slows down.)

Level 1   WB16

▶ After the count in (123123), all quietly count the beat and gently tap it on palms, noticing when the beat changes speed, and matching it.

Level 2   WB17

▶ After the count in, all clap the first beat of every bar:

1	2	3	1	2	3
👤			👤		

Level 3   WB18

▶ Perform these action patterns – one for each section. Start the section pattern after the section count in:

Section 1:

1	2	3	1	2	3
👟			👟		

x 7

Section 2:

1	2	3	1	2	3
✋		✋	✋		✋

x 7

Section 3

1	2	3	1	2	3
👟	✋	✋	👟	✋	✋

x 7

Section 4

1	2	3	1	2	3
✋		👏	👏		

x 7

Teaching tips

To help the children recognise what is happening in the music, focus on the instruments and what they are playing (panpipe playing a melody, bombo drum and shaker playing a repeated rhythm, flutes making bird sounds, claves.)

Level 2: if they find this difficult, pat the air to mark the silent beats, and listen very carefully to the speed of the beat, particularly as it speeds up and slows down.

Take care not to rush during the slow section – nor to clap too early or too late during the second and fourth sections.

Level 3: encourage the children to internalise the count.

Beat skill builder 7 ~ Beat box beats

Listen to Beat box beats

Questions you might ask

- How many beats are there to the bar? (4.)

- What do you hear after the first count in? (Four different beat box sounds; sounds which imitate a drum kit.)

- Which instruments do the sounds represent? (*tschhh* – cymbal; *dumm chhh* – bass drum and snare; *t* – hi-hat; *cheka* – shaker.)

- What do you notice about the speed of each beat box sound? (It seems like they get faster; *cheka cheka* sounds fastest.)

- Is the music getting faster? (No, the sounds all fit into the same four beats.)

What you will need

7))) WB19-24

Level 1
WB19-21

▶ After *Get ready*, all count the beat out loud and gently tap it in the palm of the hand, feeling the beat of the music (WB19).

▶ After the first count in (up to *Get ready*), all practise making the beat box sounds with voices (WB20):

– listen to the cymbal sound; copy it in the 4-beat gap;

– listen to the drum and snare sound; copy it in the 4-gap; continue by copying the hi-hat then the shaker.

Practise until confident.

▶ Repeat, but this time perform the beat box sounds *at the same time* as the track leaving a 4-beat gap after each one (WB21).

Level 2
WB21

▶ Perform the whole piece. Begin as above, then after *Get ready*:

– perform the cymbal sound; rest for four beats;

– perform the drum and snare sound; rest for four beats, and so on with the hi-hat and shaker. The complete sequence is repeated two more times.

Level 3
WB22-24

▶ Divide the class into four groups and allocate one of the sounds to each. After *Get ready*, all the groups make their sound at the same time then rest for four beats and so on to the end of the music WB22).

▶ When this is secure, swap to the next instrument each time (WB23).

	1 2 3 4	1 2 3 4	1 2 3 4	1 2 3 4	1 2 3 4
Group 1	cymbal	*silent*	drum + snare	*silent*	hi hat
Group 2	drum + snare	*silent*	hi hat	*silent*	shaker
Group 3	hi hat	*silent*	shaker	*silent*	cymbal
Group 4	shaker	*silent*	cymbal	*silent*	drum + snare

Teaching tips

Level 2/3 extension: to help the children feel how each sound seems faster than the one before, but still fits into the same four beats, perform the whole activity using body percussion in place of the beat box sounds:

– cymbal: clap;

– drum + snare: stamp + pat knees;

– hi-hat: tap finger on table;

– shaker: rub hands together.

Each sound is marking a different division of the 4-beat bar, doubling each time:

– cymbal (beats 1 and 3);

– drum + snare (1 2 3 4);

– hi hat (1+2+3+4+);

– shaker (1+++2+++3+++4+++).

The notation for this is given on WB24.

Beat skill builder 8 ~ Beat patterns

Listen to Beat patterns

Questions you might ask

- How many beats are there to the bar? (4.)
- What do you notice about the music if you tap the beat on your palms throughout? (Sometimes the music seems to be off the beat; there are places with long, sustained sounds; the sustained sounds are held for progressively longer amounts of time.)

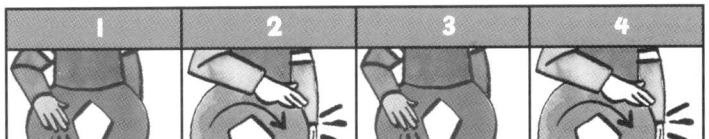

Level 1   WB25

▶ After the count in (12341234), all quietly count the beat and gently pat knees right then left with one hand. After each count of four, swap hands.

1	2	3	4

Level 2   WB26

▶ Focus on the introductory electronic voice singing this to the beat:

1	2	3	4	1	2	3	4
De da	da da	De da	da da	De da	da da	De da	doh

This 2-bar pattern recurs throughout the piece.

▶ Pat knees as above, but stop patting every time you hear the electronic voice. Join in again immediately it has finished (WB26).

Level 3   WB27-28

☐ Practise each of these action patterns (WB27).

	1	2	3	4
A				
B				
C				
D				

▶ After the count in, perform pattern A until the electronic voice signals stop, then perform pattern B, and so on. After D go back to A, and so on to the end (WB28).

Teaching tips

Level 1: encourage the children to make an arc shape as they pat from one knee to the other:

Keep the beat steady. Try not to be put off by what the music is doing. In the places where the music pauses, keep the speed steady so that when it resumes everyone is still patting in time.

Level 2: careful! – sometimes there is only a 4-beat gap between repetitions of the electronic voice.

Level 3: action patterns – to help 'feel' the beats on which there is no action, internalise the count or slightly nod the head to the beat.

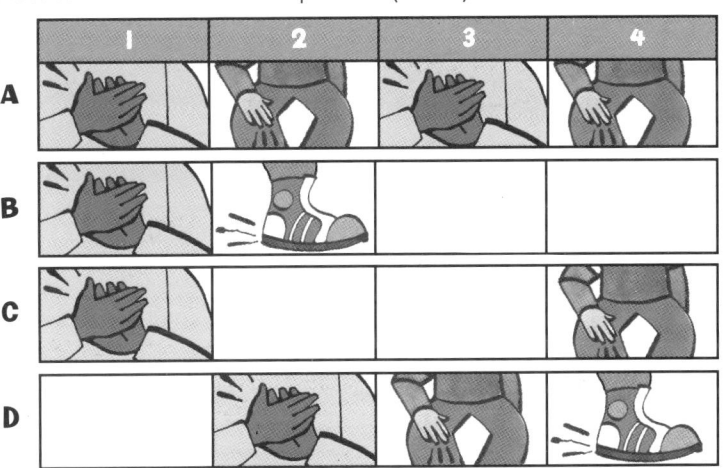

Beat skill builder 9 ~ Cyborg chase

Listen to Cyborg chase

Questions you might ask

- How many beats are there to the bar? (4.)
- Explain that the music represents a Cyborg coming to life and speeding up in stages. He moves at four different speeds within the 4-beat count. Each movement is marked by a different sound. Focus on the sounds on the counted beats – what do you hear? (Beat 1 = electronic sound; beats 1 and 3 = a buzzer; beats 1 2 3 4 = a bell; beats 1+2+3+4+ = a tapping sound.)

Level 1   WB29

▶ After the count in (12341234), all join in counting out all four beats and gently patting the beat on palms.

Level 2   WB30-32

▶ Call out the beats as demonstrated in the track (WB30), eg

1	2	3	4
One	(rest)	(rest)	(rest)

x 4

Repeat the sequence over the second half of the track.

▶ Now perform the Cyborg movements – one for each speed (WB31):

A – stamp on beat 1 (x 4 bars, alternating feet);

B – march on beats 1 and 3 (x 4 bars);

C – walk quickly on beats 1 2 3 4 (x 4 bars;

D – 'run' on the spot with small controlled steps, keeping toes on the ground, on beats 1+2+3+4+. Repeat the whole sequence.

▢ Notice how the Cyborg movements are notated in the chart, WB32, and what the notations are called:

♩   crotchet: a sound lasting one beat;

♫   two quavers equal one crotchet (it is common practice to count these out by saying 'and' [+] between each beat, eg 1+2+3+4).

𝄽   crotchet rest: rest for one beat (but don't go to sleep and forget where you are!).

Level 3   WB31

▶ Give four groups, A-D, the corresponding movement to perform. Each group performs their movement in turn during the first half of the music. In the second half, each group starts in turn, then continues their movement, so that by the end all are performing at the same time.

Teaching tips

Tempo and beat: the tempo (speed) of this music is constant, but within the 4-beat count, different speeds can be found. The beat will 'feel' slow if only the first of every four beats is emphasised. Emphasising every other beat seems twice as fast, and so on:

1   2   3   4
1   2   3   4
1   2   3   4
1+2 + 3 +4+

Level 1 and 2: encourage the children to internalise the counting of the silent beats and mark them by patting the air with both hands. Only count out the beats which have a sound/movement.

The movements will really help the children feel the acceleration, even though the basic tempo never changes.

Beat skill builder 10 ~ Rap split

Listen to Rap split

Questions you might ask

- How many beats are there to the bar? (4.)
- What do you notice about the rap words and the beat? (The rap words highlight the beat; there is one word for every beat.)
- Listen to the words. Can you remember them all?

1	2	3	4	1	2	3	4
Walk	with	me,	come	down	the	street,	And
rap	the	words	and	feel	the	beat.	
Don't	be	late,	and	don't	be	slow,	Just
move	it,	groove	it,	let	it	flow!	

- How many times is the rap performed? (Three times.)

Level 1
WB33

▶ After the count in (1234), all walk on the spot to the beat, taking one step per word. Encourage the children to make small movements, barely lifting the feet off the floor.

▶ Walk the rap again, this time performing the words as well.

Level 2
WB34

Teaching tips
Level 2: as each group reads out the words on their line of the score, it will help them if they actively feel and read the rest boxes (Walk *rest* me *rest*...)

If the children find level 2 difficult, practise each part separately without the music: group B counts 1 2 3 4 repeatedly at a slow speed, while group A say their words and vice versa.

▶ Divide into two groups, A and B, and follow the score on WB34. Both groups walk the beat on the spot while saying their part:

	1	2	3	4	1	2	3	4	
A	Walk		me		down		street,	And	▶
B		with		come		the			▶

Level 3
WB35

▶ Divide the class into four groups, A–D, and ask each to follow their part on the score on WB35.

	1	2	3	4	1	2	3	4	
A	Walk				down				▶
B		with				the			▶
C			me				street		▶
D				come				and	▶

▶ Repeat. This time everyone performs their part and walks the beat at the same time.

Beat skill builder II ~ Time change

Listen to Time change
WB36

Questions you might ask

- What do you notice about the number of beats per bar? (There are sections of 3, 4 and 5 beats per bar.)

- What do you notice about the 3-beat section? (It alternates with the 4- and 5-beat sections.)

- As you listen again, follow the diagram of the music – opposite and on WB36. What happens after the voice stops counting the beats out loud? (The same sequence keeps repeating: two bars of three, then two bars of four, two bars of three, two bars of five.)

- How does the music end? (With two bars of three.)

What you will need

Level 1
WB37

▶ After the count in (123123), all gently tap the beat on palms, noticing the changes in the count, but continuing to tap at a constant speed.

Level 2
WB38

▶ After the count in, quietly count 123123, then 12341234, then 123123 and so on. Gently tap the beat on palms as above. Emphasise the first beat by saying and tapping it slightly louder.

Level 3
WB39

▶ Perform these actions to each section.

3-beat section: x 2

4-beat section: x 2

5-beat section: x 2

Teaching tips
Level 3: 4-beat sections – encourage the children to make a definite stop to the arm movements, so that the end of the movement comes on the beat.

Beat skill builder 12 ~ Flamenco fever

What you will need

12))) WB 40-42

Listen to Flamenco fever

Questions you might ask

- What happens in the first half of the music? (There are different patterns of clapping; there is a gap after each pattern.)
- What happens in the second half of the music? (The piece repeats, but without the counting.)

Teaching tips

Beats to the bar: this piece could be considered to have four beats to the bar, but to make this exercise easier to manage, the beat has been subdivided into a count of eight half beats.

Beat and rhythm: the clapping and stamping patterns demonstrate the relationship between beat and rhythm. By playing sounds on some beats and staying silent on others, rhythm is created.

Level 1   WB40

☐ Look at the clapping patterns A–D on WB40. Practise performing each pattern without the music at a slow speed. Give a steady count in (1-8) then everyone counts to eight twice, clapping on the dots. Repeat the exercise for each pattern. Practise the patterns again at a faster pace.

▶ When this is secure, perform the patterns with the music. Listen to the pattern clapped in the first two cycles of 8, then copy-clap in the second two cycles of 8:

1	2	3	4	5	6	7	8	1	2	3	4	5	6	7	8
●		●		●		●	●								

In the second half of the music the sequence of patterns A-D repeats, but the counting disappears. Encourage the children to keep counting quietly throughout, so they do not lose their place.

At the end of the second half, simply clap the beat till the music ends.

Level 2   WB41

☐ Practise the stamping patterns, A–D, on WB41 as above.

▶ Perform the stamping patterns in the gaps after the clapping patterns. For example, listen to Clap A, then perform Stamp A, and so on.

Repeat the sequence, then finish by stamping feet on the beat until the music ends.

Level 3   WB42

▶ Perform the clapping and stamping patterns together in the gaps. Divide the class into two groups:

group 1 listens then claps patterns A–D in the gaps;

group 2 listens then stamps patterns A–D in the gaps.

Rhythm skill builder 1 ~ Pop of the peeps

Listen to Pop of the peeps

Questions you might ask

- The music is based on *Beat 1*. How many beats are there to the bar? (4.)

- The patterns of sound made by the peeps are called rhythms. What do you notice about the peep rhythms? (There are lots of different ones; each peep rhythm is heard twice with a gap afterwards, then it changes to a new one.)

What you will need

13))) WB1-3

Rhythm skill builder whiteboard numbering starts again from 1.

Level 1   WB1

▶ After the count in (12341234), copy-clap each peep rhythm in the gap.

1	2	3	4	1	2	3	4
listen to the peep rhythm				clap the peep rhythm			

Level 2   WB1

▶ After the count in, pat knees for four beats while listening to the peep rhythm then clap the rhythm in the 4-beat gap:

1	2	3	4	1	2	3	4
listen to the peep rhythm				clap the peep rhythm			

Level 3   WB1-3

▢ Complete the quiz on WB2, then display the peep rhythm chart on WB3. Practise clapping each of the peep rhythms – give a 4-beat count in.

▶ Read the rhythm from the chart as you listen, then clap it in the gap (WB3).

▶ When this is secure, tap a heel on the 2nd and 4th beats throughout. Keep tapping – read the peep rhythm then clap it in the gap (WB1).

Teaching tip

Level 3: prepare for reading the peep chart by answering the quiz questions on WB2, either as a class or individually, using print outs.

1	2	3	4	1	2	3	4
	👟		👟		👟		👟
listen to the peep rhythm				clap the peep rhythm			

Rhythm skill builder 2 ~ Taj Mahal Dancing

Teaching tip

Level 1: clapping the rhythms – the children should keep their hands held loosely together so they are always ready to clap.

Level 3: sometimes, the next finger cymbal or wood block cue will overlap with the end of clapping the previous one, but the children should try not to let this put them off. This is a very challenging exercise and may take lots of practice.

Listen to Taj Mahal Dancing

Questions you might ask

- The music is based on *Beat 2*. How many beats are there to the bar? (4.)
- What do you hear before the count in? (A finger cymbal plays a rhythm and a wood block plays another rhythm.)
- If one rhythm sounds like it is saying *Taj Ma-hal* and the other sounds like it is saying *Danc-ing*, which is which? (Finger cymbal = *Taj Ma-hal*; wood block = *Danc-ing*.)
- After the count in, do the rhythms start on the same beat of the bar each time? (No, they begin on various beats throughout the music.)
- What happens after each rhythm? (The same rhythm is clapped on the following beat.)

Level 1   WB4

▶ After the count in (12341234), say and clap *Taj Ma-hal* after each finger cymbal rhythm (at the same time as the claps) and *Danc-ing* after the wood block rhythm.

▶ Next, clap the finger cymbal and wood block rhythms, internalising the words.

Level 2   WB5

☐ All stand in a clear space and practise walking the rhythms on the spot, alternating left and right feet:

L R L	R L R	L R	R L
Taj Ma-hal	**Taj Ma-hal**	**Danc-ing**	**Danc-ing**

▶ Perform the foot rhythms; freeze in position between each rhythm.

Level 3   WB6

▶ Divide the class into two groups, A and B. After the finger cymbal, Group A claps *Taj Mahal*. Straight after this, Group B claps *Dancing*:

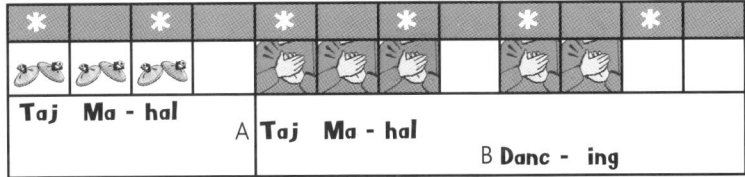

When the sound changes to wood block, the groups perform:

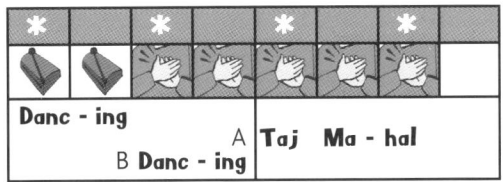

Rhythm skill builder 3 ~ Slide it

Listen to Slide it

What you will need

15))) WB 7-11

Questions you might ask

- The music is based on *Beat 3*. How many beats are there to the bar? (4.)

- What's new about this version of the music? (A low-sounding flute plays short melodies; there is a gap after each melody; each short melody has a different rhythm; each is played twice.)

Level 1   WB7

▶ After the count in (12341234), copy the rhythm of each flute melody by clapping it in the gap.

Level 2   WB8-10

☐ Show the rhythm notation of the three flute melodies, A B C (opposite and WB8). Highlight these points:

– the piece uses these three rhythms;

– the crotchet lasts one beat (page 16); the note with a hole is a minim. It lasts for two crotchet beats;

– each rhythm is played twice with a 4-beat gap afterwards.

▶ Follow the notation of the rhythms as they are played and clap them in the gaps. Can the children say how many times the flute goes through the sequence. (Three times, ending with A.)

☐ Practise the A rhythm using these actions and vocal sounds to represent the minims and crotchets (WB9). Give a 4-beat count in for each one:

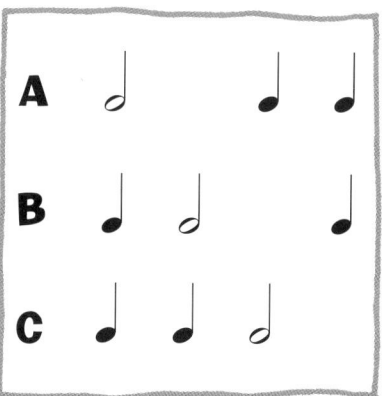

A

B

C

Teaching tip

Level 1: the children will have a tendency to rush. Counteract this by asking them to count out the beats in a whisper (12341234 etc.)

A	♩ notation	arm and clap actions
A	♩ notation	line and fist actions
A	♩ notation	shhhhh ch ch

Together, work out what the B and C rhythms would be.

▶ Perform the patterns in the gaps (WB10). Use the arm and clap actions the first time through; change to the line and fist actions the second time through; make the vocal sounds the third time, and finish with the arm and clap actions for the final A.

Level 3   WB11

▶ Clap in the gaps, but this time don't copy; clap the next rhythm instead.

Rhythm skill builder 4 ~ Have a rest

What you will need

16))) WB 12-14

Listen to Have a rest

Questions you might ask

• The piece uses fragments of Vivaldi's *Four Seasons*. How many beats are there to the bar? (2.)

• Listen to the first 55" of the track. There are two main sections. What do you notice about the sections? (The first has a melody played by a string orchestra with a drum kit accompanying – when the orchestra repeats a bit of the melody quietly, a voice counts out numbers; the second section has a rhythm, which the orchestra plays – the voice counts in the gaps after the rhythm when just the drum kit is playing.)

• Listen to the whole track. The music of the first half is repeated. What happens when the music repeats? (The counting stops; the drum kit stops during section 2. It ends with a short bit of section 1 again.)

Teaching tips

Notation: two quavers are played equally in the time of one crotchet beat:

Can the children remember hearing a rhythm before which would be notated like this? (*Taj Mahal.*)

Level 1   WB12

▶ After the first count in (1212), copy-clap the rhythm in the gap:

After the second count in, pat the rhythm on your knees throughout (no gaps). Try not to speed up or slow down. Keep steady even when there are silences.

Level 2   WB13

▶ Remind the children that a bar in this music lasts two beats – the time it takes to clap the rhythm. The counted numbers in the music mark the bars:

One			Two			Three		
1		2	1		2	1		2

▶ Practise conducting all through the music.

Level 3   WB14

▶ After the second count in, the children tap the 2-beat rhythm on their knees as above, and conduct the counted rest bars. As they conduct, the children join in counting the numbered bars in the first half, and count them on their own in the second half.

Rhythm skill builder 5 ~ Twang and crow

Listen to Twang and crow

Questions you might ask

- The music is based on *Beat 5*. How many beats to the bar are there in the different sections? (3 beats in one section, 4 beats in the other.)

- What has been added to the music? (A mouth harp – a springy, boing sound – plays rhythms with gaps afterwards in the 3-beat sections; in the 4-beat sections a cockerel 'crows' out a 'cockadoodledoo' rhythm with a gap afterwards.)

Level 1   WB15

▶ After the count in to the 3-beat section (123123), copy the mouth harp rhythms by clapping in the gap.

During the 4-beat section, copy the cockerel rhythm by saying 'cockadoodledoo' in the gap.

Level 2   WB16-17

☐ Look at the three different rhythms, A B C, used in the 3-beat sections and the rhythm for the 4-beat section (WB16).

Practise clapping and counting out rhythms A, B, C. Say 'and' (+) to mark the quavers (eg *One two and three*) and open hands to mark rests. Give a 3-beat count in so that everyone starts together.

▶ Divide the class into three groups:

Group A claps and counts out Rhythm A in the gap;

Group B claps and counts out Rhythm B in the gap;

Group C claps and counts out Rhythm C in the gap.

All groups clap and say the *cockadoodledoo* rhythm in the gap.

Level 3   WB16

▶ Everyone claps and counts out each of the A, B and C rhythms.

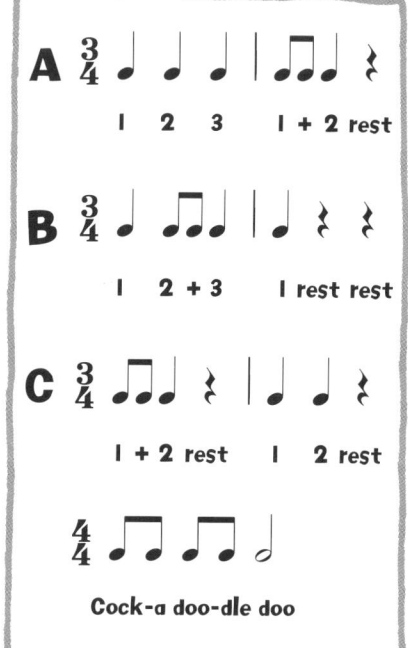

Teaching tips

Level 1: encourage the children to 'pat the air' to mark the rests physically.

Level 2: when the A B C rhythms are familiar, ask the children to say the order in which they come in each 3-beat section (WB17). Answer: ABC, CBA, CAB.

Ask the children to work out how to count out rhythm D:

D 4/4 ♫ ♫ ♩
   1 + 2 + 3 4

Listen to Andean bird dance
WB18

Questions you might ask

- The music is based on *Beat 6*. How many beats are there to the bar? (3.)
- What happens to the panpipe tune in each section? (In each section it is played at different speeds.)
- Look at the rhythm notation below (WB18). Listen to the panpipe tune during the first section – up to 27". How many times do you hear the rhythm played? (Three times.)

What you will need

18))) WB18-20

Level 1
WB18

▶ After the count in (123123), clap and count out the panpipe rhythm to the first section (up to 27").

▶ Now clap the panpipe rhythm to all the sections from beginning to end, remembering to pause at the end of each section for the count in to the next section. This time, internalise the count.

Level 2
WB19

☐ In pairs, the children practise the four rhythms opposite (WB19). One gives a count in and counts out the rhythm; the other uses body percussion to perform the rhythm, eg
A tap heel;
B clap;
C pat knees (RLRLR L);
D tap shoulders.

Come together in a sharing session and ask volunteer pairs to perform a rhythm for everyone to copy.

▶ Perform a different body percussion pattern during each section, eg Section 1 – **A**; Section 2 – **B,** etc.

Level 3
WB20

☐ Make up then practise a sequence of the A–D body percussion patterns to play during the first section, eg **A B C D A B.**

▶ Perform the sequence with the first section; then try it to each of the four sections.

▶ Now perform the sequence and panpipe rhythm together. Divide the class into two groups:

Group 1 claps the panpipe rhythm all through,

Group 2 performs the sequence.

A
I   2   3   I rest rest

B
I + 2 rest   I + 2 rest

C
I + 2 + 3   I rest rest

D
rest rest 3 +   I rest rest

Teaching tips
Level 1: encourage the children to 'pat the air' to mark the rests physically.

Listen to Beat box rhythms

Questions you might ask

- The music is based on **Beat 7**. How many beats are there to the bar? (4.)
- What does the beginning of the track demonstrate? (Four different rhythms using vocal sounds that imitate a drum kit.)
- What happens after the 'get ready' signal? (The vocal sounds are heard one after the other; there is a 4-beat gap after each sound.)

What you will need

19))) WB 21-24

Level 1

WB21-22

▶ After the first count in (12341234), learn the rhythms by copying each one in the 4-beat gap (WB21).

▶ Perform the whole piece. Begin as above, then after **Get ready**, perform rhythm 1, rest for four beats, perform rhythm 2, rest for four beats and so on. Repeat the whole sequence two more times (WB22).

Level 2

WB23

▶ Divide the class into four groups and give each group one of the rhythms to perform. After **Get ready**, all the groups perform their rhythms in the first four beats, then rest for four beats, and so on.

tschh   tschh   tschh

dum dum   chh   dum   chh chh

t t   t t

che-ka che-ka chek   che-ka che-ka che-ka   chek

	1 2 3 4	1 2 3 4	1 2 3 4	1 2 3 4	1 2 3 4
Group 1	cymbal	*silent*	cymbal	*silent*	cymbal
Group 2	bass + snare	*silent*	bass + snare	*silent*	bass + snare
Group 3	hi hat	*silent*	hi hat	*silent*	hi hat
Group 4	shaker	*silent*	shaker	*silent*	shaker

Level 3

WB 24

▶ If the children find level 2 comfortable, extend them further with this version:

	1 2 3 4	1 2 3 4	1 2 3 4	1 2 3 4	1 2 3 4
Group 1	cymbal	*silent*	bass + snare	*silent*	hi hat
Group 2	bass + snare	*silent*	hi hat	*silent*	shaker
Group 3	hi hat	*silent*	shaker	*silent*	cymbal
Group 4	shaker	*silent*	cymbal	*silent*	bass + snare

Teaching tips

Level 1: test the children on their understanding of time values, eg
- How many quavers can you play in the time of a crotchet? (2)
- How many semiquavers can you play in the time of a quaver? (2)
- How many semiquavers can you fit into 4 crotchet beats? (4x4=16)

Rhythm skill builder 8 ~ Syncopate it

What you will need

20))) WB25

Listen to Syncopate it

Questions you might ask

- The music is based on *Beat 8*. How many beats are there to the bar? (4.)

- What do you notice if you tap the beat throughout? (Sometimes the music feels off beat – it's harder to the tap the beat during these bits.)

Level 1

WB25

☐ Compare the two rhythms below (WB25). Rhythm A falls entirely on the main four beats:

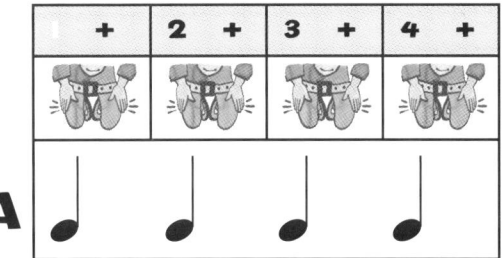

Rhythm B is syncopated, which means 'off the beat'. The first note falls on beat 1, but the others fall in between the main beats (1 + + + +):

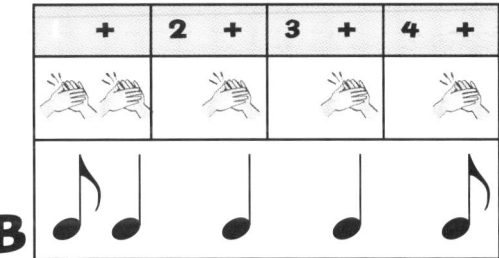

☐ Practise this. Give a count in of 1+2+3+4+, then tap four bars of Rhythm A on your knees. Change to Rhythm B for four bars. Change back to A. Keep alternating them until this is really secure.

▶ After the 'De da da da' music and count in, pat four bars of Rhythm A on knees then clap four bars of Rhythm B. Keep swapping till the music ends.

Level 2

▶ Repeat the activity. This time keep the main beat throughout by tapping it with heel or toe – even when clapping the syncopated rhythm.

Level 3

▶ Reverse the rhythms. Start by clapping Rhythm B then swap to patting Rhythm A, and so on.

Rhythm skill builder 9 ~ Cyborg attack

Listen to Cyborg attack

What you will need

21))) WB 26-28

Questions you might ask

- The music is based on *Beat 9*. How many beats are there to the bar? (4.)

- What do the two synthesisers play? (Sythesiser 1 plays a short rhythm twice then synthesiser 2 copies.)

- How many different rhythms do they play? (Four, then the whole sequence is repeated.)

- Do the rhythms fall on the beat or off the beat? (They are a mixture; the last one is very off beat/syncopated; only one rhythm is on the beat all through.)

Level 1

WB26

▶ Copy synthesiser 1 by clapping along with synthesiser 2.

Level 2

WB27-28

☐ Show the four rhythms opposite (WB27). Introduce:
half beat quaver note ♪   half beat quaver rest ⅞

▶ Ask the children to look at the notation (WB27) and as they listen, call out the letter of the rhythm being played, ie:

A	A	B	B	C	C	D	D
synth 1	synth 2	synth 1	synth 2	synth 1	synth 2	synth 1	synth 2

x 2

☐ Clap the rhythms without the track. Divide into two groups. Give a count in then:

Group 1 counts **1 + 2 + 3 + 4 +** steadily and repeatedly;

Group 2 claps Rhythm A repeatedly.

▶ Now listen to synthesiser 1 then all count and clap along with synthesiser 2.

Level 3

▶ Revise the movements for Cyborg chase (page 16). Then in two groups, perform the movements and clap the rhythms:

	A	A	B	B	C	C	D	D
	synth 1	synth 2	synth 1	synth 2	synth 1	synth 2	synth 1	synth 2
Group 1		Clap A		Clap B		Clap C		Clap D
Group 2	Stamp	Stamp	March	March	Walk	Walk	Run	Run

▶ For a more challenging performance, each person performs the movements and rhythms simultaneously.

Teaching tips

Level 2: use the quiz questions (WB28) during level 2 to focus everyone on the notation and how it works:

1. What is the rhythmic difference between bar 1 and bar 2 in rhythm A? (None. The rhythm is the same. They may sound different, but this is because the rhythm is played on different pitches in bar 2.)
2. Which rhythm begins on the beat? (Rhythm C.)
3. Which rhythms begin 'off the beat'? (Rhythms A, B and D.)
4. Which is the most syncopated rhythm? (Rhythm D.)

Give individuals and pairs opportunities to practise counting and clapping out the rhythms.

Level 3: when the children are secure with performing the movements and clapped rhythms in two groups, challenge everyone to move and clap the rhythms at the same time (encourage them to internalise the count).

Rhythm skill builder 10 ~ Word walk

Listen to Word walk

Questions you might ask

- The music is based on *Beat 10*. How many beats are there to the bar? (4.)
- How many times is the rap performed? (Three times.)
- Four word rhythms are given at the beginning of the piece. When do you hear them again? (During the rap; when the rap is played the first and second times, you hear the word rhythms.)

Look at   me

Walk -ing   walk - ing

Walk   slow

Hip   jig - gle

Teaching tip

Level 2: if the children find this difficult, divide into four groups and give each group one rhythm to chant. The groups chant in the order shown in sequence 2.
Level 3 extension: perform the sequences in different combinations. Decide as a class how you will order and combine the sequences during the rap.

Level 1   WB29-30

▶ After the first count in (12341234), listen to the word rhythms then say them along with the quieter voice (WB29).

▶ After the second count in, perform the word rhythms along with the voice – twice each – during the first run through of the rap (WB29).

☐ Show sequence 1 (WB30). This is the sequence the children have just performed. It shows how the rhythms are organised in relation to the rap.

▶ Listen again, following the sequence as the music plays.

Level 2   WB31

☐ Show sequence 2. This is how the word rhythms are ordered and combined during the second run through of the rap.

▶ Ask the children to follow the sequence as they listen.

☐ Choose a small group of children to give a slow, steady count in (12341234) then say the rap. Everyone else performs the word rhythms as shown in sequence 2.

▶ Perform sequences 1 and 2 up to speed with the track.

Level 3   WB30-32

☐ Show sequence 3 (WB32). The word rhythms are ordered and combined differently again. Practise the new sequence as above until really secure.

▶ Perform all three sequences one after another (WB30-32).

Rhythm skill builder II ~ Three four five

Listen to Three four five

What you will need

23))) WB 33-35

Questions you might ask

- The music is based on *Beat 11*, but this time there are only three sections. How many beats are there to the bar in each section? (The first section has 3 beats per bar, the second has 4 beats per bar and the third has 5 beats per bar.)

- How many rhythms do the synthesisers play in the 3-beat section? (One.) The melody notes change, but the rhythm always stays the same. Is this true for the 4-beat and 5-beat sections? (Yes; each has one rhythm.)

- Two different synthesiser sounds are used. What do they play? (The first plays the rhythm and the second one copies it.)

Level 1   WB33

▶ After the count in (123123), listen to the first synthesiser, then clap the rhythm when the second synthesiser copies.

Do the same for each section.

Level 2   WB34

☐ Show the notation opposite (WB34) – the three rhythms in the piece.

▶ Clap the rhythms with synthesiser 2, but this time count out the beats saying 'and' (+) to mark the quavers. Encourage the children to internalise the count when synthesiser 1 plays.

Level 3   WB35

▶ Perform the rhythms in two groups using body percussion:

Group 1 perform the body percussion along with synthesiser 1;

Group 2 copy group 1 along with synthesiser 2.

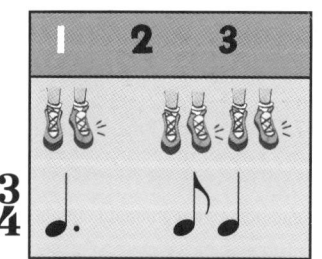

Teaching tip

Level 1: if the children find it difficult (especially in the 5-beat section) ask them to count out the beats as synthesiser 1 plays and then clap.

Level 2: each rhythm begins with a dotted crotchet. A dot after a note adds half the note's value, so the dotted crotchet lasts for one and a half beats.

Rhythm skill builder 12 ~ Castanet cuisine

Listen to Castanet cuisine

What you will need

24))) WB36-39

Questions you might ask

- The music is based on *Beat 12* but the beat is not subdivided into eight this time. How many beats are there to the bar? (4.)

- The first half of the track demonstrates eight different castanet rhythms linked to a Spanish food word or phrase. How many times is each rhythm heard? (Twice.)

- What happens in the second half of the piece? (Food rhythms are joined together to make longer rhythms.)

Level 1   WB36

▶ After the count in (12341234), listen to the castanets then say and clap the word rhythms (*wine*, *tapas*, *oranges*, *chick peas*, *red pepper*, *carajillo*, *fish paella*, *olives 'n' wine*) in the gaps. Each word rhythm is played twice.

In the second half of the piece, copy-clap the longer rhythms in the gaps.

Level 2   WB37-38

▢ Show the class the notation for the food rhythms (WB37). Now ask them to look at the rhythms from the second half of the piece (WB38). Each rhythm is a combination of the food rhythms, eg

or-an-ges or-an-ges or-an-ges wine

Divide the class into nine groups and give each group a rhythm from WB38. Each group works out the words or phrases that go with the notation and rehearses their rhythm by chanting and clapping it.

▶ Perform the rhythms with the track. Everyone copies the food rhythms in the first half as before. In the second half, the nine groups in order, chant and clap their rhythms in the gaps.

Level 3   WB39

▶ Repeat the exercise for level 2, but this time each group makes up their own combination of the food rhythms to play in the gaps. Remind the children that only rhythms that add up to four beats will fit!

wine

tapas

oranges

chick peas

red pepper

carajillo

fish paella

olives 'n' wine

Pitch skill builder I ~ Line by line

Listen to Line by line

Questions you might ask

- The music is based on *Rhythm 1*. How many beats are there to the bar? (4.)

- What do the two synthesisers play? (They copy each other; sometimes they make one long, low-sounding note, sometimes it's high; other times they make sounds which slide up or slide down in pitch, or both.)

- If we call the lines and curves of the sounds, which the synthesisers play, pitch shapes, how many different shapes can you hear? (Six not including copies – one low, one high, one slide up, one slide down, one up and down, one down and up.)

What you will need

25))) WB1-2

Pitch skill builder whiteboard numbering starts again from 1.

Level 1   WB1

▶ After the count in (12341234), copy-sing each pitch shape to 'Ooo' along with synthesiser 2.

Level 2   WB2

☐ Show these pictures of the pitch shapes (WB2):

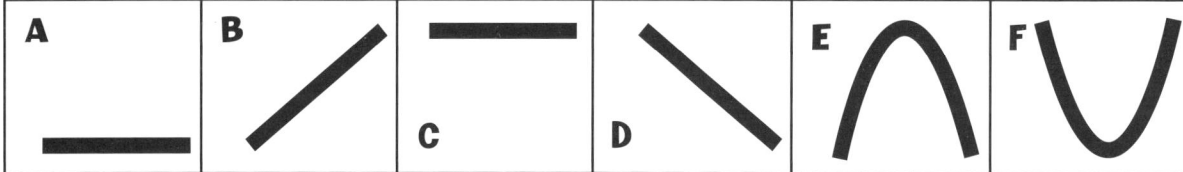

▶ Synthesisers 1 and 2 play A-F twice through in order, then a third time jumbled up. Ask the children to listen and:

　1. follow the pitch shapes as they are played in order A–F twice through.

　2. work out the order of the third play through. (Answer: A D F C B E).

▶ Now ask the children to follow the shapes as synthesiser 1 plays, and copy-sing along with synthesiser 2.

Level 3   WB2

☐ Practise drawing each pitch shape in the air, eg

▶ Listen to the shape synthesiser 1 plays, then draw the shape when synthesiser 2 copies it.

▶ Copy-sing and draw the shapes at the same time.

Teaching tip
Level 3: encourage the children to listen carefully in the third play through to make sure they draw the correct shape.

Pitch skill builder 2 ~ Ping pong pitch

What you will need

26))) WB 3-5

Listen to Ping pong pitch

Questions you might ask

- The music is based on *Rhythm 2*. How many beats are there to the bar? (4.)

- What do you hear at the beginning? (A sitar plays four different pitches in order from low to high; a singer and a flute copy the notes.)

- After the count in, what do the sitar, singer and flute play? (The sitar plays the *Taj Mahal* rhythm on different notes/pitches; the singer and flute copy on the next beat; then the sitar plays *Taj Mahal* again and the singer and flute copy; later the sitar plays the *Dancing* rhythm on different pitches and is copied on the next beat each time.)

- Do you notice anything special about the notes which the sitar uses when it plays the *Taj Mahal* and *Dancing* rhythms? (It uses different mixtures of the four notes played at the beginning of the piece.)

Level 1
WB3-4

▶ Before the count in, the sitar plays four notes – join in singing them to 'ah' as the flute copies (WB3).

▶ After the count in (12341234), imitate the sitar, singing the same notes and matching word rhythm (*Taj Mahal* or *Dancing*) on the next beat (WB4).

Level 2
WB5

☐ Show how the note patterns are represented on WB5:

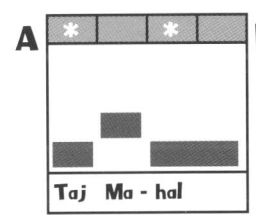
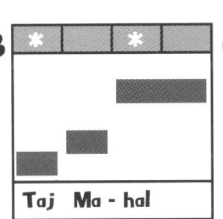
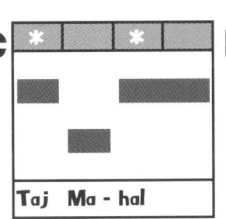
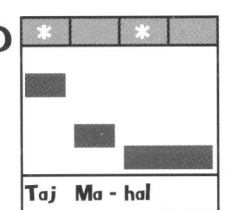
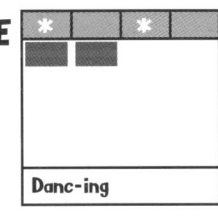

A: Taj Ma - hal
B: Taj Ma - hal
C: Taj Ma - hal
D: Taj Ma - hal
E: Danc-ing

▶ Follow each pattern as it is played the first time through then ask:
– How many different pitches does pattern A use? (2.) Repeat the question for the other patterns. (B=3, C=2, D=3 and E =1).

Teaching tip
Level 2: there are many more things to notice in the patterns. Make up your own questions, eg which pattern has notes which start low and end high?

▶ Ask the children to think about these questions as they listen again:

– the *Taj Mahal* patterns are played A B C D. When they return later in the music, what order do they play in? (A C D B).

– what happens to the *Dancing* note pattern each time it is played? (It starts on the highest pitch, then is played lower each time; next time it starts low and gets higher each time, ending on the highest pitch.)

Level 3
WB5

▶ Sing with the flute as before. This time read the note patterns and draw the patterns in the air (as opposite) to show the way the pitch moves.

Pitch skill builder 3 ~ Smooth it

Listen to Smooth it

What you will need

27))) WB 6-7

Questions you might ask

- The music is based on *Rhythm 3*. How many beats are there to the bar? (4.)

- What do you notice about what the flute plays? (It plays short tunes/note patterns which are each repeated after a gap; there are three different patterns; the whole sequence of patterns is played three times through, ending with the very first pattern played a fourth time.)

Level 1
WB6

▶ After the count in (12341234), copy the flute by singing in the gap. Use a different vocal sound for each play through of the whole sequence:

First time through sing 'ah'

Second time through sing 'yo'

Third time through sing 'hee'

Last pattern sing 'ah'

Teaching tip
Encourage the children to sustain each note for its full length, singing smoothly.

Level 2
WB7

☐ Show how the note patterns are represented on WB7:

A			
1	**2**	**3**	**4**

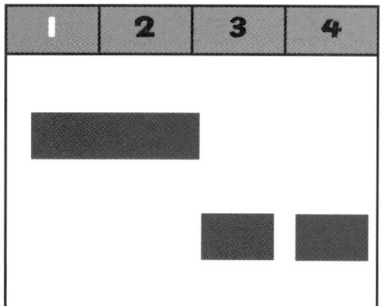

B			
1	**2**	**3**	**4**

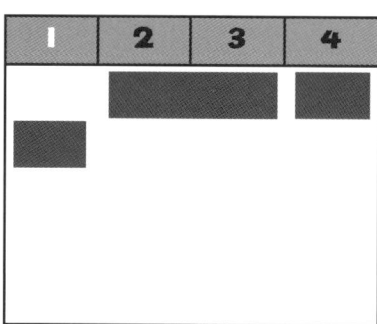

C			
1	**2**	**3**	**4**

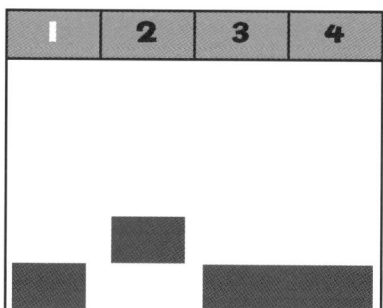

▶ Ask the children to think about these questions as they listen again:

- Which pattern uses the highest pitch?
- Which pattern uses the lowest pitch?
- Which has the biggest leap in pitch?

Level 3
WB7

▶ Repeat level 1, but as they sing ask the children to follow the notation (WB7):

▶ Draw the patterns in the air as you sing (see page 32) to show the way the pitch moves.

Pitch skill builder 4 ~ Pom pom pom

Listen to Pom pom pom

Teaching tip

Remember to conduct steadily during long periods of silence to keep in time.

Questions you might ask

- The music is based on **Rhythm 4**. How many beats are there to the bar? (2.)
- The music uses fragments of Vivaldi's *Four Seasons*, with added brass and percussion sounds. What do you notice about the music the brass instruments play? (They play three different patterns of notes; they all play the same rhythm – *pom pom pom*.)
- How many different pitches are there for the brass to play? (Only two: one higher-pitched note; one lower-pitched note.)
- What are the three patterns? (*High high high; high low high; low low low.*)

Level 1   WB8

▶ After the first count in (1212), listen to each ***Pom pom pom*** pattern then copy along with the voices. Each pattern is repeated.

Level 2   WB9-10

▢ Show the notations of the X, Y, Z patterns (WB9). Divide into three groups and allocate each a pattern to practise.

▶ After the second count in, perform this sequence of the patterns along with the orchestra (WB10):

X Y X Y X Z *(repeat)*

X Y X Y X Z Y *(repeat)*

Z *(count four bars rest)*

Z *(count two bars rest)*

Z *(count one bar rest)*

Z *(count five bars rest)*

Repeat the whole sequence for the second half of the music. Ask the children how the piece ends. (The second line is performed once.)

▶ Swap groups around and repeat the activity.

Level 3   WB10

▶ Everyone sings all the note patterns in the sequence shown in level 2.

X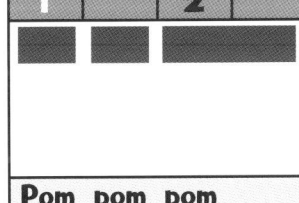

Y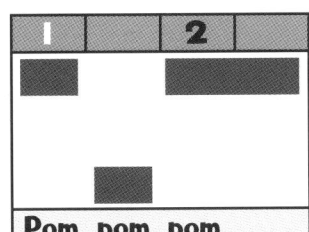

Z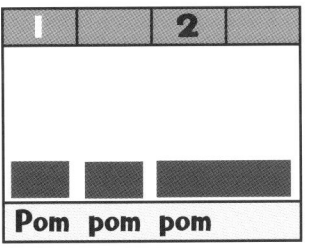

Pitch skill builder 5 ~ Chicken pets

Listen to Chicken pets

What you will need

29))) | WB11-14

Questions you might ask

- The music is based on *Rhythm 5*. How many beats are there to the bar in each section? (3, 4, 3, 4, 3.)

- What happens before the count in? (Someone sings a tune with these words: *Come my chicken pets*, *Peck peck 'n' peck peck*, *Time to go walkies*; a flute copies each phrase of the tune.)

- What happens after the count in? (During the 3-beat sections, the tune is played on harmonica not sung; the phrases are in a different order each time; in the 4-beat section there is a cockadoodledoo phrase.)

Level 1
WB11-12

▶ Before the count in, copy-sing the song phrases (WB11). Practise until this is really secure.

▶ Look at the note patterns on WB12. Copy-sing the A, B, and C song phrases before the count in, following the notation.

▶ After the count in (123123), the A, B and C phrases in the 3-beat section are reordered each time. The children need to listen carefully to the harmonica to determine which phrase to sing in the gaps (WB12). Copy-sing the *cockadoodle doo* phrase in the 4-beat section.

Level 2

▶ Sing in two parts. Divide the class into two group. After the count in, during the first 3-beat section:

Group 1 sing along with each phrase, repeating them in the gaps;
Group 2 repeatedly sings *Come my chicken pets* throughout the section (six times in all).

▶ Swap groups and repeat the exercise with a different repeated phrase:
Peck peck 'n' peck peck   or   *Time to go walkies*

Level 3
WB13-14

▶ Divide into three groups and give each group a phrase:

A   **Come my chicken pets**

B   **Peck peck 'n' peck peck**

C   **Time to go walkies**

Ask each group to work out the letter names of their notes by referring to the note finder diagram (opposite and WB13).

▶ Each group sings their phrase in the corresponding gap, but instead of singing the words they sing the letter names of the notes (WB14), eg

A   **Come my chicken pets** = G   B B A G

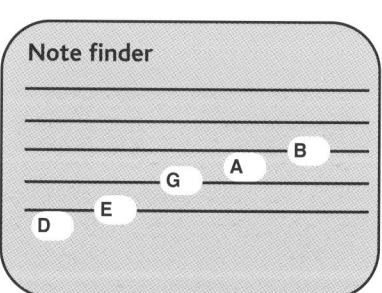

Note finder

D   E   G   A   B

Teaching tip
WB13 shows the note positions on a stave and WB14 provides the answers.

Pitch skill builder 6 ~ Andean bird song

What you will need

30))) · WB15-17

Listen to Andean bird song

WB15

▶ As they listen, ask the children to follow the written music on WB15.

Questions you might ask

- The music is based on *Rhythm 6*. How many beats are there to the bar? (3.)

- What happens to the song after it is heard in the first section of the music? (It is played three more times by the panpipes at different speeds – tempi.)

- What do the grey lines above the notes show? (The shape of the melody phrases; the shape you get if you draw the sounds in the air or if you join the notes 'dot to dot'.)

Level 1

WB15

▶ After the count in (123123), join in with the singer in the slow section. Afterwards, ask the children to say:

– What the difference is between the notes they sing for *Watch it* and the notes for *Vanish*. (*Watch it* starts high and leaps down; *Vanish* does the opposite.)

– What the difference is between the notes they sing for *Pretty bird* each time. (They are always the same; the last time, the word 'fly' is added on a lower pitch.)

– What other similarities and differences they notice in the melody.

Level 2

WB15

▶ When the children are really familiar with it, sing the song in all the sections: slow, speeding up, fast, slowing down.

Level 3

WB16-17

☐ Notice that in the written music on WB16, every other bar is numbered. Using the note finder, work out the starting note for the numbered bars. (E, D, E, D, C, D, E.)

▶ Divide into two groups to sing in two parts (WB17):

Group 1 sing the song as normal;

Group 2 sing the words in the numbered bars to the starting note, eg

last bar

E E E_____   D D D_____   E_____

In the sky_____   Cir - cle high_____   Fly._____

Note finder

```
_____
_____
_____
_____
           D        E
 - C -
```

Pitch skill builder 7 ~ Beat box toonz

Listen to Beat box toonz

What you will need

31))) | WB18-22

Questions you might ask

- The music is based on *Rhythm 7*. How many beats are there to the bar? (4.)
- How many different phrases (toonz) does the singer perform? (Four.)
- Do all the toonz start on beat 1? (The third toon starts on beat 2.)
- What words does the singer use? (Scat sounds: 1 *Oh hi ho*, 2 *Dum dum doo dum doo doo*, 3 *Doo wop doo wop*, 4 *Dabadaba doo daba dabadaba doo*.)

Level 1   WB18-19

▶ Before *Get ready*, listen to each toon then copy-sing it in the counted 4-beat gap (WB18). Each toon is repeated.

▶ Look at the patterns on WB19. Copy-sing the toonz again, drawing the shape of each toon in the air (WB19).

Level 2   WB20

▶ Divide the class into four groups and allot each group a toon. Before *Get ready*, each group copies its corresponding toon. After *Get ready*, the four groups perform in this order twice through:

Gp 1		Gp 2		Gp 3		Gp 4	
Toon 1	*rest*	Toon 2	*rest*	Toon 3	*rest*	Toon 4	*rest*

Teaching tip

Level 1: the note patterns are shown on WB19. Encourage the children to focus on the noteheads in order to see the pitch shape.

Level 2: repeat the activity letting the groups try a different toon each time.

Level 2/3: encourage the children to sustain each note for the full length of the note, singing smoothly.

Level 3   WB21-22

▶ After *Get ready*, the groups start the toonz one at a time, building up till all are performing at the same time (WB21):

Gp 1	Gp 2	Gp 3	Gp 4
Toon 1			→
	Toon 2		→
		Toon 3	→
			Toon 4 →

▶ Next, try performing the toonz at the same time (WB22):

All		All		All		All	
Toonz 1-4	*rest*	Toonz 1-4	*rest*	Toonz 1-4	*rest*	Toonz 1-4	*rest*

Pitch skill builder 8 ~ Martians

Listen to Martians

Questions you might ask

- The music is based on *Rhythm 8*. How many beats are there to the bar? (4.)

- The three riffs have words sung to them. What are they? (1 *Greetings from the Martian people*; 2 *I'm a spaceman and I come in peace*; 3 *Zoo za za za za zoo za za za za*.)

- Which riff is on the beat and which riffs are syncopated? (1 is on the beat; 2 and 3 are syncopated.)

Level 1
WB23

▶ After the first count in (12341234), listen to the three sung riffs and copy-sing them in the gap.

Level 2
WB24

▶ After the second count in, perform the riffs throughout the track. Careful – there are no gaps! Sing them in this order:

1 **Greetings from the Martian people.**
2 **I'm a space man and I come in peace.**
3 **Zoo za za za za zoo za za za za.**
3 **Zoo za za za za zoo za za za za.**

Stop singing whenever the *De da da da* music plays. When it stops, begin again.

Level 3
WB25

▶ Invent 'alien' hand signals to show the pitch shape of each riff then perform them with the music.

When completing this activity, some children will find it useful to refer to WB25 which shows the staff notation for each riff.

▶ Perform one of the riffs as an ostinato (repeating pattern). After the second count in, sing riff 1 (and make the alien signals) repeatedly throughout. Only stop singing when the *De da da da* music is playing.

▶ Repeat the exercise with riff 3, then try riff 2. The children will find it difficult at first to sing their riff repeatedly while hearing the others, but encourage them to 'boldly sing were no one has sung before.'

Teaching tip

Level 2: if the children find it difficult swapping from one riff to the next, divide them into three groups and allocate them one riff each.

Level 3: WB25 gives the staff notation for the riffs should you wish to use it.

Pitch skill builder 9 ~ Cyborg hide and seek

Listen to Cyborg hide and seek

What you will need

33))) WB 26-29

Questions you might ask

- The music is based on on *Rhythm 9*. How many beats are there to the bar? (4.)

- How many different word phrases are sung? (Four but each is repeated; 1 *I know you're hiding*; 2 *I'm gonna find you now*; 3 *Coming closer*; 4 *Tick, tick, you're it!*)

- What happens to each phrase when it is repeated? (It has the same shape but it is repeated at a lower pitch.)

Level 1   WB26

▶ After the count in (12341234), listen to the singer and synthesiser 1 and copy-sing with synthesiser 2. When the music repeats and the voice drops out, listen to synthesiser 1 and sing along with synthesiser 2.

Level 2   WB27

▶ Show the pitch shapes A-E on WB27. Ask the children to match them with the Cyborg word phrases. (Phrase E is a trick phrase and is not used.)

Level 3   WB28-29

▶ Sing in two parts. Divide the class into two groups:

Group 1 sings each phrase as before through to the end.

Group 2 repeats each phrase at the same pitch.

etc

Synth							
Gp 1							
Gp 2							

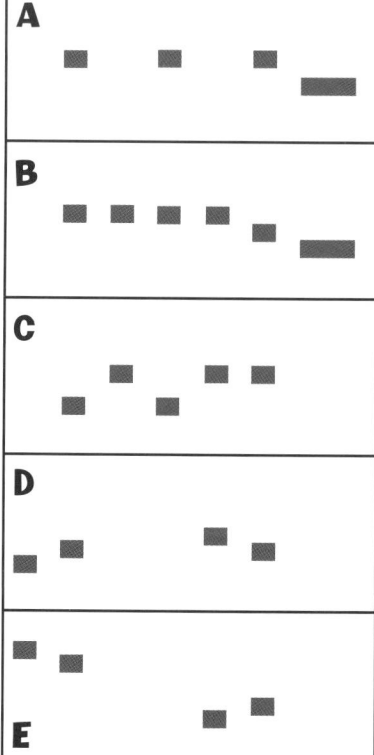

Teaching tip

Level 2: remember that each phrase is repeated at a lower pitch, but it is still the same shape.

Level 3: WB 29 gives the phrases in staff notation if you wish to use it.

Pitch skill builder 10 ~ Hill walk

Listen to Hill walk

Questions you might ask

- The music is based on *Rhythm 10*. How many beats are there to the bar? (4.)
- How many times is the rap performed? (Three times.)
- After the count in, what do you notice about the music the sythesiser plays? (It plays a different melody each time the rap is spoken; the first and third melodies are the same.)

Level 1   WB30

▶ Look at the notation of the sythesiser part. After the count in (12341234), follow the synthesiser melody as it plays over the spoken rap. Notice that each line of the spoken rap takes up two rectangles of the notation.

Line 1:   **Walk with me, come down the street, And**
Line 2:   **rap the words and feel the beat.**
Line 3:   **Don't be late and don't be slow, Just**
Line 4:   **move it, groove it, let it flow!**

▶ After the count in, sing the synthesiser melodies to **Ah**, following the notation.

Level 2   WB31

▶ Instead of singing 'ah', sing the rap, fitting the words to the synthesiser melody, eg

rap the words and...

down the street, And

Walk with me, come

Teaching tip

Level 2: it helps if the children are really familiar with the rap words so they can concentrate on following the pitch shapes as they sing.

Level 3

▶ Sing in two parts. Divide the class into two groups:

Group 1 sing as normal
Group 2 sing the first synthesiser melody for every repeat of the rap.

Pitch skill builder II ~ Chemistry

Listen to Chemistry

What you will need

35))) | WB32-35

Questions you might ask

• The music is based on *Rhythm 11*. How many beats are there to the bar? (Section 1 has 3 beats to the bar; section 2 has 4; section 3 has 5.)

• What do you notice about the synthesiser melodies before the count in? (The rhythms match the singer's words – *chemistry*; *bubbles in a tube*; *magnify molecules*.)

Level 1   WB32

▶ Before the count in, join in with the voice and synthesiser 2 as they copy synthesiser 1, singing:

  Che - mis - try

  Bub - bles in a tube

  Mag - ni - fy mo -le - cules

Level 2   WB 33-34

▶ Repeat the activity for Level 1, but this time look at WB33, which shows the patterns notated like this:

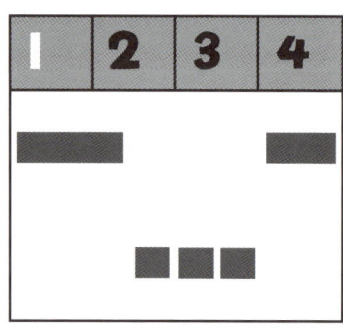

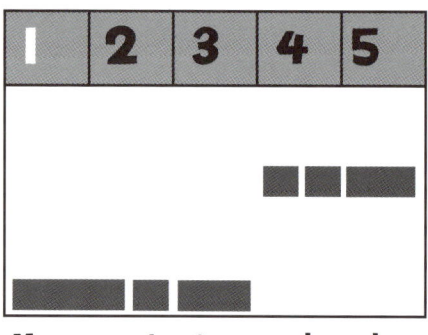

After the 3-beat count in (123123), there are lots of different note patterns for **Chemistry**. Listen out for the notated **Chemistry** pattern shown on WB33. When the children hear it played by synthesiser 1 they sing it with synthesiser 2 (WB34).

Do the same after the 4-beat count in with **Bubbles in a tube**. After the 5-beat count in, identify and sing the notated **Magnify molecules**.

Level 3   WB 35

▶ Sing all the note patterns. Follow the notation on WB35. After each count in, listen to the first synthesiser play the note patterns in turn and then join in singing when the second synthesiser copies.

Pitch skill builder 12 ~ Food fiesta

What you will need

36))) WB36-38

Listen to Food fiesta

Questions you might ask

- The music is based on *Rhythm 12*. How many beats are there to the bar? (4.)
- What do you hear the trumpet and strings play? (The strings copy what the trumpet plays; the trumpet plays lots of different note patterns; the whole thing is played twice through, finishing with a second repeat of one pattern.)
- How many different note patterns does the trumpet play? (Five.)
- How long does each note pattern last? (8 beats; two bars.)

Level 1
WB36

▶ After the count in (12341234), copy-sing the trumpet note patterns to 'la' along with the strings.

Level 2
WB37

▶ Show the children the notation on WB37. These are the trumpet patterns but they are not in the right order. Listen, then identify the correct order. (B A E D x 2, ending C):

Level 3
WB38

☐ Look at WB38 and practise singing the words to the trumpet phrases.

▶ Listen to the trumpet. Sing the matching phrase along with the strings.

A

Dance and drink, then you dine.

B

Food   Fi - es - ta!

C

Sleep,   si - es - ta!

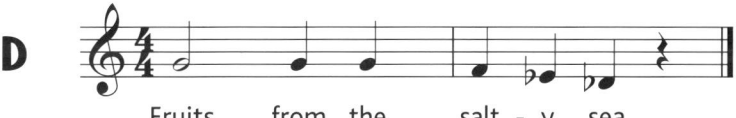

D

Fruits   from   the   salt - y   sea.

E

Fla - vours of   the   sun.

Celebrate! ~ Number song

Listen to Number song
track 1, WB1

Listen to track 1. When the song is familiar, listen again and clap on each number 1 and number 5. Focus the children on what the numbers might mean and ask these questions (WB1):

Questions you might ask

- Which number is the lowest in pitch, and which is the highest? (Number 1; number 8.)

- How many different pitches are there in the song? (There are eight; one for each number.)

- How are the numbers between 1 and 8 organised? (In order; they are each one note higher than the previous; like a ladder.)

- What is a musical ladder called? (A scale.) Which notes sound the most important notes in this musical ladder? (Lowest/highest; numbers 1 and 8.)

What you will need

1-5))) | WB1-8

- Printouts for individuals to work with.

- Prepared tuned percussion or keyboards with stickered notes:

| 1 C | 2 D | 3 E | 4 F | 5 G | 6 A | 7 B | 8 C' |

Number song beats
track 2, WB2

1. The song has four beats to the bar:

1	2	3	4
One two	three four	five...	

Listen to track 2 and join in counting the beat – not the song words – all the way through the song.

2. Repeat. This time add a knee slap on beat 1 each time you say it.

1	2	3	4

Number song rhythms
WB3

1. Give pairs a copy of WB3 printout and a prepared tuned instrument (notes CDEFG). The children play a question and answer game based on this rhythm and these pitches from the song:

Player 1 (Question)	Player 2 (Answer)
♩ ♩ ♩ ♩ ♩	♩ ♩ ♩ ♩ ♩
1 2 3 4 5	5 4 3 2 1

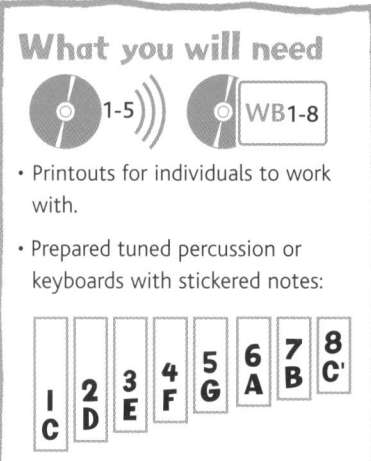

Number song pitches
track 1/3-4, WB1/4-5

1. Sing the song along with track 1 (WB1). When the children are confident, sing it without the CD and teach these body movements:

   – on 8, hands above head

   – on 7, touch head

   – on 6, touch shoulders

   – on 5, touch middle;

   – on 4, touch thighs;

   – on 3, touch knees;

   – on 2, touch shins;

   – on 1, touch toes.

2. Practise singing with the actions, slowly at first then gradually getting up to the speed of the CD. Try performing the song with actions only, internalising the melody and words.

3. Sing pitch numbers 1, 5, 6, 7 and 8 out loud: internalise the other numbers (track 3, WB4).

   When everyone can manage this well, sing pitch numbers 2, 3, 4, 6, 7 and 8 out loud, internalising 1 and 5 (track 4, WB5).

   Divide into two groups:

   Group 1 sings numbers 1 and 5 (plus 6, 7, 8);

   Group 2 sings numbers 2, 3 and 4 (plus 6, 7, 8).

Number song performance
track 5, WB6

1. With or without backing track 5, sing the song as a round in two groups, practising until you can sing it three times through: 1st time with actions and voices, 2nd time with actions only, 3rd time with voices only:

   Group 1 begins;

   Group 2 begins when Group 1 reaches the line beginning 1 5 4 5.

2. Add an ostinato on tuned percussion (notes CGABC', WB6). Play the ostinato twice for each repeat of the song.

Teaching tips

Listen: show the children the notation of the song if it helps them to visualise the number 'code'.

Number song beats: focus carefully to avoid muddling the numbers of the pitches with the numbers of the beats.

Number song pitches extension: divide into two groups and sing the version of the song given on WB7 in which the order of the numbers is changed. When everyone is confident with this new version, try this! A soloist takes the part of Group 2 and sings 234 in any order.

Optional staff notation for the song is given on WB8.

1	2	3	4	1	2	3	4
𝅗𝅥		𝅗𝅥		𝅗𝅥		𝅗𝅥	
1		5		5		1	
♩	♩	♩	♩	♩	♩	♫	♩
8	7	6	5	8	7	6 7	8

Celebrate! ~ Hi lo chicka lo

Listen to Hi lo chicka lo
track 6

What you will need

6-8))) WB 9-13

- Untuned percussion instruments.

Hi lo chicka lo beats
track 6-7, WB9-10

1. Play track 6 and all improvise a funky chicken walk in time to the 3-beat section. When the 4-beat song section starts, all stand in one place and tap knees to the slow steady beat while the song plays (WB9).

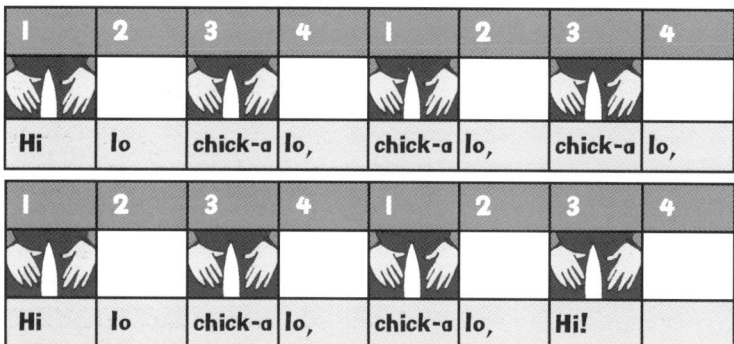

1	2	3	4	1	2	3	4
Hi	lo	chick-a	lo,	chick-a	lo,	chick-a	lo,

1	2	3	4	1	2	3	4
Hi	lo	chick-a	lo,	chick-a	lo,	Hi!	

2. Play track 7 and quietly clap the fast beat, joining in with the song as soon as it becomes familiar (WB10).

3. Ask individuals to demonstrate their chicken walks and together choose two walks for everyone to perform. Divide into two groups, each allocated one of the walks.

   Play track 6. As the groups circulate, performing the two walks, each individual finds a partner from the opposite group. When the 4-beat section starts, the pairs stand facing each other, singing the song and clapping each other's hands to the fast beat of the song. After the song, the pairs part and recirculate in search of a new partner.

Hi lo chicka lo rhythms
WB11

1. Show the children the rhythms and words on WB11 and together identify how they match up.

2. Working in pairs, each with a different percussion instrument:

   Player 1 plays the fast beat of the song;
   Player 2 taps the rhythms.

   Swap parts. Try playing the rhythms against the slow beat, which you tapped on your knees.

cluck

Hi lo chicka lo pitches
track 6

1. Revise the song, clapping the fast beat, then divide into facing pairs.

2. Clasp left hands together as though shaking hands then place them back to back (palms facing out). Explain that on the words:

   hi – the pairs clap each other's right hands in the space above their left hands;

   lo – they clap each other's right hands in the space below their left hands;

   chick – each person claps their *own* left hand.

3. Perform the song slowly with the actions, until all the pairs are performing the actions correctly along with the song.

   What do the children notice about the action pattern they are making with their hands? (It moves high, low and in-between; it copies the pitches in the song.)

4. Play track 6. In the groups from the beat activity, perform the chicken walk to locate a partner. At the end of the chicken walk everyone faces the person nearest to them and performs the song with the clapping actions.

Hi lo chicka lo pitch notation
WB12

1. Draw a horizontal line on a board which everyone can see. Explain that the line represents the children's left hands – the in-between pitch in the song.

2. Decide as a class how to draw the melody of the song (an example is given on WB12). When you are happy with the result, sing the song, following the notation by pointing to each note as you sing it.

3. Invite an individual to rearrange the notation to make a new order of high/low pitches around the middle pitch. Sing the new melody.

Teaching tip
Pitch notation: as an alternative to drawing the pitches, lay a skipping rope in a line on the floor, and use round floor markers to show the pitches.

The staff notation of the song is given on WB13, should you wish to use it.

Hi lo chicka lo mix
track 8

1. Listen to track 8. Can the children say what happens in the 4-beat sections this time? (The *Hi lo chicka lo* pitches are played in different patterns. Each new pattern is played twice.)

2. As the track plays again, all listen to, then copy the pitch shape in the air with right hands. (They may use their extended left hand to mark the middle pitch.)

   Ask individuals to demonstrate some of the new patterns and notate them using the simple notation above.

3. In groups as before, perform the chicken walk, locate a partner and together listen to, then perform the new pitch actions.

   For extra trickiness, ask a small, separate group of children to sing the original song while the others are performing the new pitch actions. Harder still – ask everyone to sing the original song while performing the new patterns!

Celebrate! ~ Bodywork

Listen to Bodywork
track 9

Questions you might ask

• Why is this piece called 'Bodywork'? (It is performed using body percussion.)

• Which parts of the body can you hear? (Feet, hands, and chest.)

• Can you hear one body or two? (Two bodies/groups playing one part each.)

What you will need

9-13))) WB14-15

Bodywork beats
track 13

1. All stand in a circle. Play track 13 and ask the class to step on the spot from right to left on the main beat, clapping once on beat 1:

1	2	3	4
👏			
👟	👟	👟	👟

2. When everyone can feel the steady beat and the first strong beat, select one child, A, to start this game. Play track 13 again:

Count in (12341234) – Child A establishes eye contact with Child B on the other side of the circle;

First beat of the music – Child A steps across the circle taking eight paces/beats to reach and stand next to Child B;

All count 12341234 – Child B makes eye contact with Child C;

Next strong beat – Child B starts stepping eight paces across the ring to stand next to Child C, and so on.

Bodywork notation
track 10-11, WB14

1. Display the notation of *Bodywork*. There is a stave for each performer. The notes at the bottom of the stave are stamped, notes at the top are clapped and notes on the middle line are tapped on the chest.

2. Play track 10, following the notation for player 1 together. Follow the notation for player 2 with track 11. Join in as the parts become familiar.

Questions you might ask

• In the first line of notation, are the parts the same or different? (Same.) Do they come together again anywhere? (In bars 10 and 16.)

• How many times is the rhythm pattern of the first bar played in each part? (Four times.)

• What rhythm is played by tapping the chest? (The fast notes; semiquavers in bars 5,7,9,11,13,15.) Is there any other chest rhythm? (No.)

Teaching tips

Bodywork beats: when the game is secure, introduce variations, eg
– when Child A arrives on beat 8, Child B immediately leaves on the next beat 1, having already established eye contact with Child C;
– start two or three children at the same time;
– devise a funny walk to the steady beat.

Bodywork notation: ensure that the children understand that the notation does not show pitch; it shows the rhythms and it differentiates between the three parts of the body. In this it is similar to the way drum music is notated.

Bodywork rhythms extension: choose a leader to display the rhythm cards to the class one by one. The class respond with the appropriate action, repeating it for as long as the card is displayed.

Further ideas
• Add movement to the piece as appropriate to its mood and character.
• Find three different sounds to play eg bubble wrap, empty tube cartons and tin cans.
• Compose your own *Bodywork*.

Bodywork rhythms

track 12, WB14-15

1. Remind the children of the rhythm played on the chest and show them the rhythm card for it (WB15). Play track 12 (both parts at slow tempo) and invite all the children to join in with the chest rhythm when they hear it.

   Divide the class into two groups to perform the chest rhythm in two parts while track 12 plays (WB14):

   Group 1 follows part 1 and performs the chest rhythm;

   Group 2 follows part 2 and performs the chest rhythm.

   Did everyone manage to tap in the right place?

2. Remind the children of the rhythm stamped and clapped in bar 1 and elsewhere and show them the rhythm card for it (WB15). Play track 12 and invite all the children to join in with this rhythm when it occurs.

   Divide the class into two groups and perform the stamp/clap rhythm while track 12 plays (WB14):

   Group 1 follows part 1 and performs the rhythm;

   Group 2 follows part 2 and performs the rhythm.

   Did everyone manage to stamp and clap in the right place?

3. When both rhythms are secure, perform the piece again in two groups, joining in with both rhythms while track 12 plays (WB14).

Perform Bodywork

track 13, WB14

1. Working in pairs with the notation, learn the whole of part 1. Suggest to the pairs that they practise the rhythms in two-bar sections without the CD, following the notation. When they can do this, perform four-bar sections, finally putting the whole part together.

2. Now as a class, perform part 1 (with backing track 13 for support if you wish).

3. Repeat stages 1 and 2 with part 2. Finally, divide into two groups and perform both parts of *Bodywork* together (with or without the backing).

   Consider these questions to refine your performance:

   – How can dynamics be added to the piece? Which sections of the music could be loud and which quiet? What about the ending? Should it be loud or quiet? Fade out or build?

   – Why is tempo important in the piece? (Try different speeds. Which is the most effective for a controlled but interesting performance?)

Bodywork pitches

1. Divide the class into small groups and ask each to create their own vocal version of the piece, using three different pitches. The vocal sounds could be unique or could reflect the sounds of clapping, stamping and patting.

Celebrate! ~ Hey, Mr Miller

Listen to Hey, Mr Miller
track 14

As they listen to track 14, ask the children to focus on the steady beat and notice the way that some of the rhythms 'swing' against it.

What you will need

14-18))) WB16-17

Questions you might ask

• Who was the Mr Miller referred to in the title? (Glenn Miller, 1904 –1944, was a well-known American band leader.)

• Why is the last part of the song sung to 'ba ba ba ba' syllables? (It is imitating the sound of a trumpet.)

Hey, Mr Miller beats
track 15, WB16

1. Play track 15 and ask the children to focus on the words of the song and what they are about:

Hey, Mr Miller,
What a swing that you bring to the band,
Hey, Mr Miller,
What a swing that you bring to the band.

With your trombone and your saxophone,
You can hear it all through the land,
With your trombone and your saxophone,
You can hear it all through the land.

Ba ba ba ba ba ba ba ba daba daba
Daba daba daba, da ba doo wah!
Ba ba ba ba ba ba ba ba daba daba
Daba daba daba, da ba doo wah!

(The song is about Glenn Miller's dance band and refers to some of the instruments.)

2. Ask each child to choose either a trombone, a trumpet or saxophone to air play. Play track 15; everyone swings in time with the beat throughout.

When everyone is comfortable keeping the beat, divide into three groups:

Group 1 – plays saxophone in section 1 *Hey Mr Miller... to the band*.

Group 2 – plays trombone in section 2 *With your... through the land*.

Group 3 – plays trumpet in section 3 *Ba ba ba... doo wah!*

Play track 15. As soon as the introduction ends, group 1 stand up energetically and keep the beat using a saxophone movement. They sit down and are followed by group 2. Group 3 don't keep the beat – instead they air play the *Ba ba ba ba* rhythm.

Hey, Mr Miller rhythms
track 16-17

1. An important feature of this style of music is swinging the beat. Use track 16 to practise copy-singing (to 'ba') the swing rhythms played by the instruments.

2. Familiarise the class with track 17, in which double bass and percussion play the accompaniment. Working in small groups, the children use rhythms they have learnt above, to work out a short rhythm-only section to fit the steady bass part. Use vocal sounds, body percussion or untuned percussion.

If working without the track, one person in each group must be responsible for keeping a steady beat that everyone can work over. Make sure they give a clear count in. Practise playing the same rhythms in unison (at the same time) or combining different ones.

3. Share each group's work, using track 17 for accompaniment.

Teaching tips

Use an internet search engine to find footage of Glenn Miller's band playing 'In the mood' to see and hear the *Ba ba ba ba* quotation in *Hey, Mr Miller*.

The Glenn Miller sound included trombones, saxophones, trumpets, double bass, drum kit and sometimes clarinets and singers.

Hey Mr Miller beats: Group 2 action comes in on a silent first beat. Ask them to beat time quietly throughout section 1, ready to stand up and take over without missing a beat in section 2.

Hey Mr Miller pitches: when singing the round, remind group 2 that the first note they sing is silent for group 1. Don't be put off!

Staff notation is given on WB17.

Hey, Mr Miller pitches
track 15/18, WB16

1. Use track 15 to learn the song melody and words thoroughly. Notice how in each of the three sections, the words and melody are repeated.

2. Divide the class into two groups and sing the song as a round. When group 1 reach the second section, group 2 start. When this is secure, sing the round in three groups. Use track 18 for backing.

3. Make some performing decisions:

– one person (or one from each group) beats time throughout;

– you might choreograph the instrument movements you worked on earlier so that everyone swings and points their air instruments in the same direction within their groups;

– decide whether or not to use the backing track;

– consider where to use the rhythm compositions;

– consider an introduction to the song;

– how will you end? Perhaps fade out when the class has sung round the sections twice, or organise for everyone to finish with the trumpet section.

Celebrate! ~ Yonder come day

Listen to Yonder come day
track 19

As they listen to track 19, encourage the class to start to feel the steady beat and familiarise themselves with the song.

What you will need

 19-23))) WB18-19

- A large clear space or hall for movement work.

Yonder beats
track 20, WB18-19

1. Play track 20 and together count out the beats as you listen (WB18-19):

1	2	3	4	1	2	3	4
Walk		that		road			

Use track 20 to teach the class Part 1, stepping left and right on the spot.

2. When this is secure, the children stand one behind the other in four straight lines, two of which face the opposite direction. This time, as they perform along with the CD, everyone steps forward and after two repeats of 'walk that road', turn about and walk back the other way.

Decide on different directions to travel and create a new formation.

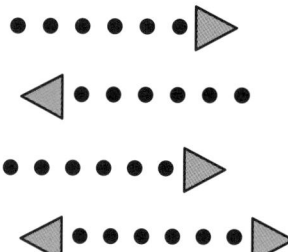

Yonder rhythms
track 21, WB18-19

1. Use track 21 to practise Part 2, which is spoken (WB18):

> **Trees are green and the air is sweet,**
> **The good earth is singin' underneath my feet.**
> **I'll point my feet down the freedom line,**
> **Walkin that road I'm feelin' fine, Yeah!** *(Repeat)*

2. Show the class the notation of Part 2 (WB19). Notice the syncopated rhythm at the end of each line, eg *air is sweet*.

Yonder pitches

track 22, WB18-19

1. Use track 22 to practise Part 3, which is sung (WB18):

> Yonder come day, day is a-breakin'
> Yonder come day, oh my soul,
> Yonder come day, day is a'breakin'
> Sun is a'risin' in my soul.

2. Show the class the notation of Part 3 (WB19) and follow it while listening to track 22.

Questions you might ask

- What do you notice about the melody and rhythm on the words, 'Yonder come day' each time? (The tune and rhythm are the same each time.)
- Is the tune the same anywhere else? (The tune is the same when the words 'day is a-breakin'' and 'sun is a-risin'' are sung.)

3. Practise Part 3 until everyone is singing it securely and confidently.

Perform Yonder come day track 19/23, WB18-19

1. Divide the class into three groups and allocate one part to each. Listen to CD track 19 again.

Questions you might ask

- How are the three parts organised in this performance? (Part 1 is performed four times first; Part 2 is performed once while Part 1 continues, then Part 3 is sung once while Parts 1 and 2 continue.)

2. Using track 23 as a backing track if you wish, perform the song in three parts as above, or in an arrangement of the children's own devising.

Teaching tips

Yonder come day rhythms: encourage the children to relax into the rhythms to give it a happy, free feeling.

Performance: encourage the children to make as creative an arrangement as they like; some will be learning instruments which might be included; others may like to devise a set of dance moves based on the formations explored earlier. Aim to perform without the backing track.

Some children will find it easy and helpful to perform the actions of Part 1 at the same time as Part 2/3. Encourage everyone to do this if they can.

Celebrate! ~ Saint train swing sing

Listen to Saint train swing sing track 24-25

Without revealing the title of any of the songs, listen to track 24.

What you will need

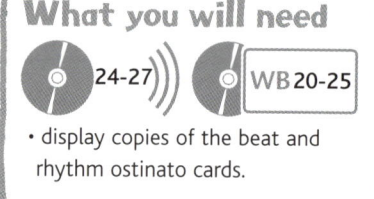 24-27)) WB 20-25

• display copies of the beat and rhythm ostinato cards.

• a few untuned percussion instruments.

Questions you might ask

• Do you recognise any of the songs? (*Swing low sweet chariot*; *This train is bound for glory*; *Oh when the saints go marching in*; *I'm gonna sing sing sing*.)

• What do they all have in common? (They are all spirituals; they all fit the same steady beat.)

• How many beats are there to the bar? (4.)

Now listen to track 25.

Questions you might ask

• What happens in the music this time? (All the songs are sung at the same time.)

• Which song starts first – listen really carefully? (*Oh when the saints*.) Which starts last? (*This train*.)

• What do you notice about the ending? (Everyone sings the same note.)

Saint train swing sing beats track 24, WB20-21

1. Count the beat throughout as you listen to track 24:

1	2	3	4	1	2	3	4
Swing	low			sweet	cha	- ri-	ot_____	

Sing the songs till they are secure then add these actions:

Swing low – swimming action, palms down, pushing forward on 1;

This train – piston movement on beats 1 and 3;

Oh when the saints – jaunty walk, stepping on every beat (keep toes on the ground and lift heels high);

I'm gonna sing – clap on beats 2 and 4 (wave hands open on 1 and 3).

2. Show the children the four beat cards (WB21) and together identify which action matches each card, eg the walking action for *Oh when the saints* matches the card with four crotchet beats.

   Ask a volunteer to repeat a steady count of four. You or another volunteer display one of the cards; the children respond with the appropriate action.

3. When all the actions and songs are firmly established, all sing the songs with track 24, but respond with the action indicated by the card held up, eg the swim card with *Oh when the saints*, or the pistons card with *I'm gonna sing*.

Swing low

This train

Oh when the saints

I'm gonna sing sing sing

Saint train swing sing rhythms track 24/26, WB22

1. Use track 26 to teach each of these rhythmic ostinatos, saying and clapping each until they are secure:

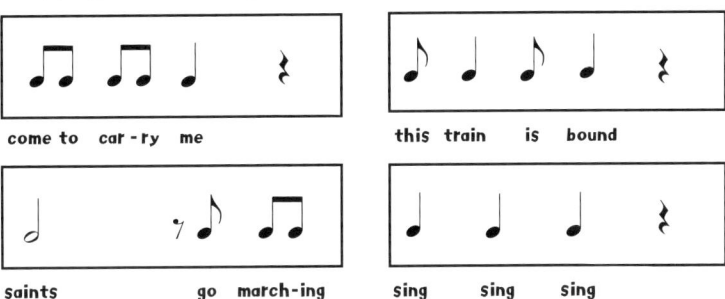

When all the rhythms are firmly established, play track 24; all clap the ostinato for each song. You or a volunteer can hold up the rhythm cards in turn as a reminder. Next sing and clap at the same time.

2. Divide into four groups – one for each song – and give one or two children from each group untuned percussion instruments with which to play the ostinato for their song as the others perform it.

3. If everyone is managing to sing and clap the ostinatos confidently, extend them further by holding up the cards in a different order to the songs – you might even change the card midway through a song.

Saint train swing sing pitch track 27-28, WB23-25

1. Ask the children to focus on the beginning of each song (WB24).

Questions you might ask

- Which two songs start on the same note? (*Swing low* and *I'm gonna sing*; they start on the note F sharp.)
- Which song begins on the first beat of the first full bar? (*This train.*)
- Which three songs have the same note on the first beat of the first full bar? (*Swing low*; *This train*; *I'm gonna sing*; the note is D.)
- Which note does *Oh when the saints* begin on? (It begins on the note D.)

2. Show the count in for the songs on WB23 and ask the children to sing the begining of each in turn. Practise counting in the opening of each song with track 27. Listen to then copy each opening.

3. When the counting in is secure, divide into four groups and sing the songs all together. You might try all at once as in track 25, or building the songs up one by one.

4. Use track 28 as a backing to your own arrangement of the songs. Decide together how you will build up your arrangement using actions and ostinatos and combining the songs in a vibrant, exciting order.

Teaching tip

Check that the class understand something of the origin of spirituals and the meaning of the words.

Some word phrases are real tongue twisters (*Aint takin none but the righteous and the holy*). Spend a little time practising tricky phrases to improve clarity.

Getting the songs started together is good practice for the children's rhythmic development. Backing track 28 includes a bell sound giving four beats to cue the beginning of the songs.

Celebrate! ~ Ayelevi

Listen to Ayelevi

track 29

Explain that this is a call and response, greeting song from Ghana. Encourage the children to move to the beat as they listen to track 29.

Questions you might ask

- How does the music encourage you to join in? (It sounds happy; it makes you want to move; it has a strong beat.)

- What do you notice about the music during the syllables *pa-pa a-*? (It sounds off-beat; it has a different rhythm from the rest of the song.)

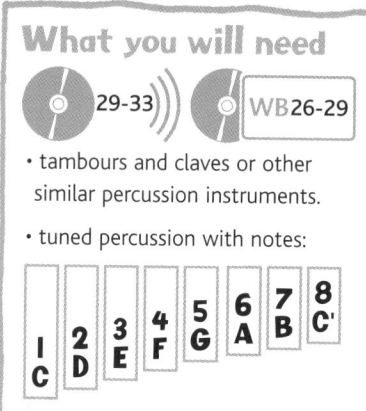

What you will need

29-33)))   WB 26-29

- tambours and claves or other similar percussion instruments.

- tuned percussion with notes:

1 C	2 D	3 E	4 F	5 G	6 A	7 B	8 C'

Ayelevi beats

track 29-30, WB26

1. Stand in a circle. Play track 29, all moving to the beat however it is felt. Ask individuals to demonstrate where they feel the beat of the song to be; there is more than one possibility (see Teaching tips).

2. Play track 30, all clapping on beats 1 and 2 – the main beats the children will be working with (WB26):

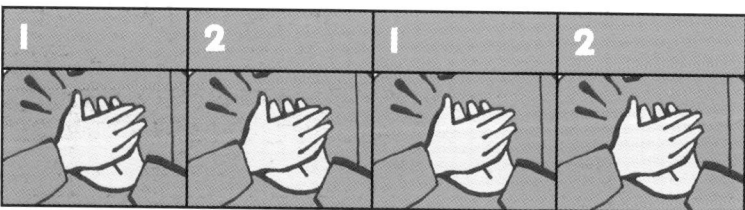

Check that everyone is able to continue clapping a steady two beats through *pa-pa a-* (the second clap falls between *-pa* and *a-*).

3. Practise joining in with the response on track 29 while clapping the beat:

   Ah ah mi do papa ayelevi.

4. When this is secure, join in with the call as well, still clapping the beat:

   Ayelevi me kulo mi do papa ayelevi.

   Sing the song without the CD, clapping the beat. Invite individuals to sing the solo call whilst the rest of the class sing the response.

Questions you might ask

- What do you notice about the last note of the call and the first note of the response? (The response starts one pitch lower than the ending note of the call; it helps us come in on the right note.)

 Music Express EXTRA: Developing Music Skills © 2007 A & C Black Publishers Ltd

Ayelevi rhythms

track 31, WB27

1. Stand in a circle and play track 31. On the words 'Step IN', the children step forward from their right foot onto their left foot, moving the whole weight of the body onto the forward foot and leaning right into the beat.

2. Now add the clapping pattern – clap clap clap (WB27):

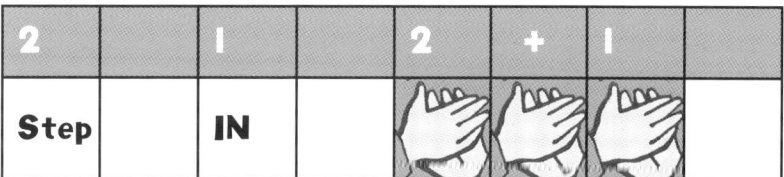

2		1		2	+	1	
Step		IN					

3. Ask the children to say if the first step falls on the strongest beat. (No. The second step falls on beat 1.) Explain that the first step of the pattern is made on an up beat.

4. When this is confident, transfer the two patterns to untuned percussion. Select two small groups to play while the others sing, clap and step:

   Group 1 plays the stepping pattern on tambours;

   Group 2 plays the clapping pattern on claves.

5. Perform the song in a circle, moving clockwise instead of facing into the centre. The percussion groups might be positioned inside the circle.

Ayelevi pitches

track 32-33, WB28-29

1. Invite a small group of children to add this tuned percussion part (WB28):

2	1	2	1	2	1	2	1	2
	C'	C'	C'	B	B	B	A	A	A	G	G	G
A -	ye - le -	vi	me	ku - lo	mi do	pa - pa	a -	ye - le -	vi

1	2	1	2	1	2	1	2
F	F	F	E	E	E	D	D	D	C	C	C
Ah	-	ah	mi do	pa - pa	a -	ye - le -	vi

2. Notice how the tuned part starts on the highest-sounding note, and drops in pitch one note at a time. Now ask individuals to show with their bodies how they can mirror this descending pattern, eg

   – perform the three claps high in the air then gradually lower with each repeat;

   – move their bodies lower as they step forward each time.

3. Ask the class to organise a performance which uses all they have learnt. How creative can the class be in structuring their performance? There are many possibilities. Use backing track 33 or your own arrangement.

Teaching tips

Ayalevi beats: when moving to track 29, some children will want to move on beat 1, others on beats 1 and 2; some may feel the fast 1+2+ beat.

Ayalevi rhythms: the song begins on the beat before the first strong beat of the bar (A– *ye*...). This is called an anacrusis. Many songs begin like this, eg *I'm gonna sing* (page 54). The 'Step IN' pattern also starts on an upbeat (Step) and moves on to the downbeat (IN).

The tuned and untuned parts can be heard on CD track 32. Listen carefully! The clapping pattern and the tuned ostinato rhythms overlap.

Staff notation is given on WB29.

Celebrate! melody lines

Number song

anon

1 2 3 4 5   5 4 3 2 1

*

1 5 4 5 3 5 2 5   1 5 4 5 3 2 1

1 2 3 4 5   5 4 3 2 1

1 5 4 5 3 5 2 5   1 5 4 5 6 7 8

* *entry point for round*

Hi lo chicka lo

traditional clapping game

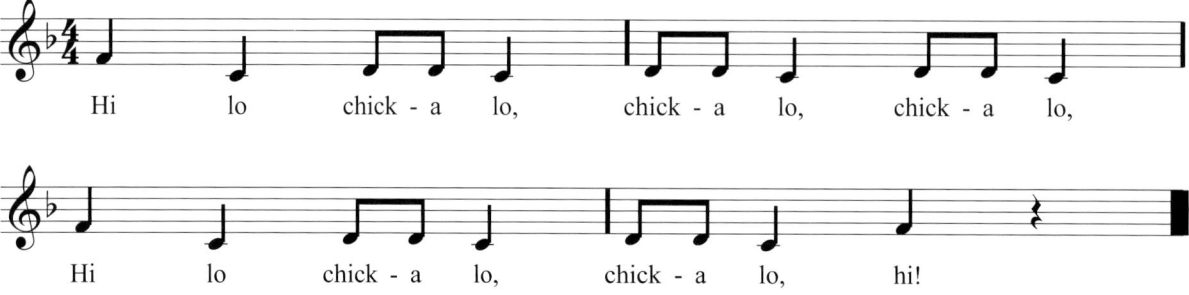

Hi   lo   chick - a   lo,   chick - a   lo,   chick - a   lo,

Hi   lo   chick - a   lo,   chick - a   lo,   hi!

Music Express EXTRA: Developing Music Skills © 2007 A & C Black Publishers Ltd

Bodywork

Jessica Berners

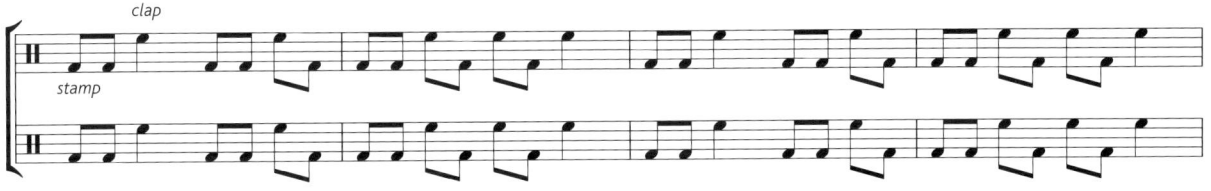

notes on the bottom space of the stave are stamped; notes on the top space are clapped; notes on the middle line are tapped on shoulders or chest

Celebrate! melody lines

Hey, Mr Miller

David Machell (sections 1-2), Joe Garland (section 3)

Section 1

Hey, Mis - ter Mil - ler, What a swing that you bring to the band,

Hey, Mis - ter Mil - ler, What a swing that you bring to the band,___ With your

Section 2

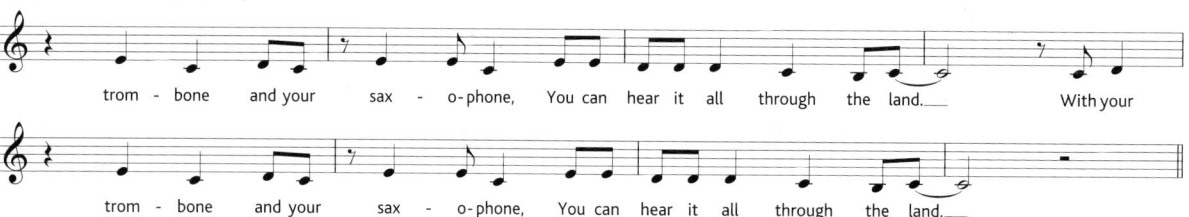

trom - bone and your sax - o - phone, You can hear it all through the land.___ With your

trom - bone and your sax - o - phone, You can hear it all through the land.___

Section 3

Ba ba ba ba ba ba ba ba da ba da ba Da ba da ba ba ba Da___ ba doo wah!___

Ba ba ba ba ba ba ba ba da ba da ba Da ba da ba ba ba Da___ ba doo wah!___

Yonder come day

traditional: adapted by Leonora Davies from an arrangement by Judith Cook Tucker

Part 1: repeat throughout

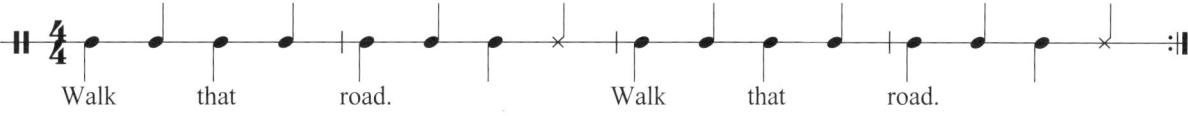

Walk   that   road.   Walk   that   road.

Part 2

Trees are green and the air is sweet. The good earth is sing-in' un-der-neath my feet. I'll

point my feet down that free-dom line. Walk-in' that road I'm feel-in' fine. Yeah.

Part 3

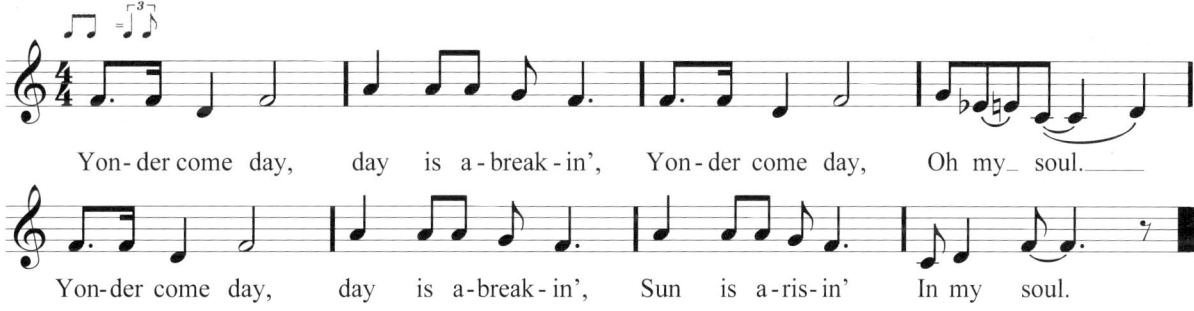

Yon-der come day, day is a-break-in', Yon-der come day, Oh my soul.

Yon-der come day, day is a-break-in', Sun is a-ris-in' In my soul.

Saint train swing sing

traditional

Four partner songs: sing one after the other or in any combination

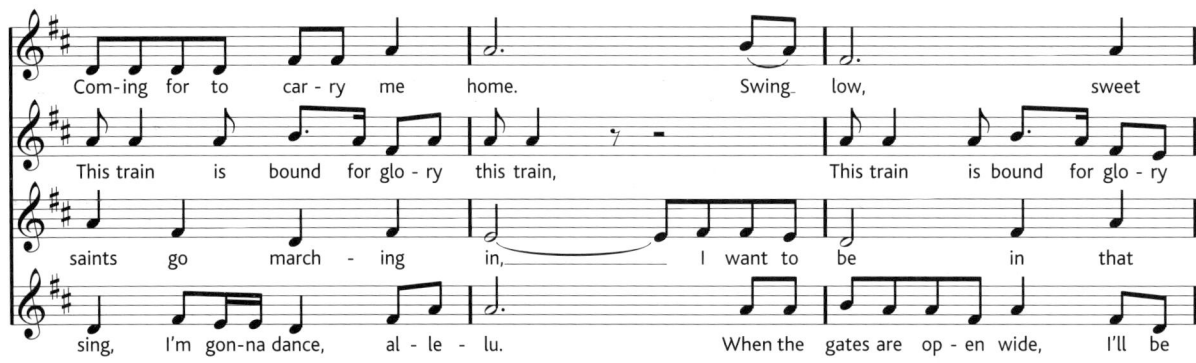

Ayelevi

traditional Ghanaian greeting song (call and response)

Acknowledgements

The following have kindly granted their permission for the use of copyright material included in this pack:

Bodywork by Jessica Berners © 2007 Jessica Berners. Used with kind permission.

In the mood (quoted in *Hey, Mr Miller*), words by Andy Razaf, music by Joe Garland © 1939 Shapiro Bernstein & Co. Inc, USA, Peter Maurice Music Co Ltd, London WC2H 0QY. Reproduced by permission of International Music Publications Ltd (a trading name of Faber Music Ltd). All Rights Reserved

Hey, Mister Miller by David Machell © 2007 David Machell. Used with kind permission.

Yonder come day traditional; arrangement adapted by Leonora Davies from an arrangement by Judith Cook Tucker.

Number round, **Saints train swing sing**, **Hi lo chicka lo**, **Ayalevi** are arranged from traditional by A&C Black. All arrangements © 2007 A&C Black Publishers Ltd.

The authors and publishers would like to thank the following for their generous assistance and contributions to this pack: Helen MacGregor for contributing the idea for *Hi lo chicka lo*; Alex Chadwick (trumpet), Chris Hatton (clarinet), Sophie Pike (trombone) for their performances on *Hey, Mr Miller*; Bobby Gargrave, Erika Jenkins, Harriet Lowe and Jeanne Roberts.

Every effort has been made to trace and acknowledge copyright owners. If any right has been omitted, the publishers offer their apologies and will rectify this in subsequent editions following notification.

First published 2007
by A&C Black Publishers Ltd
38 Soho Square, London W1D 3HB
© 2007

ISBN 978-07136-8574-9

Printed in Great Britain by Martins the Printers, Berwick upon Tweed.

Text © 2007 Stephen Chadwick and Maureen Hanke
Music (Skill builder tracks 1-36) © 2007 Stephen Chadwick
Illustrations © 2007 Alison Dexter
Sound recording © 2007 A&C Black
Cover image by James Watson © 2007 A&C Black

Edited and developed by Sheena Roberts
Designed by Fiona Grant
Music setting by MusicSet 2000
Songs performed by Em Whitfield
Sound engineering by Stephen Chadwick
CD/CD-ROM post production by Sound Recording Technology

This book is produced using paper that is made from wood grown in managed, sustainable forests. It is natural, renewable and recyclable. The logging and manufacturing processes conform to the environmental regulations of the country of origin.

A CIP catalogue record for this book is available from the British Library.